CW00801988

ACTION

Also by Robert McKee

Story: Substance, Structure, Style and the Principles of Screenwriting

Dialogue: The Art of Verbal Action for Page, Stage and Screen

Character: The Art of Role and Cast Design for Page, Stage and Screen

Storynomics
with Thomas Gerace

ACTION

The Art of Excitement for Screen, Page, and Game

BY

ROBERT McKEE

AND

BASSIM EL-WAKIL

ILLUSTRATIONS BY OLIVER BROWN

METHUEN

ACTION
Published by Methuen in 2022

1

Methuen Publishing Ltd
Orchard House, Railway Street
Slingsby, York YO62 4AN

Methuen Publishing Ltd Reg. No. 03543167

Illustrations by Oliver Brown

A CIP catalogue record for this book is available
from the British Library

ISBN: 978 0 413 77850 5

Typeset by SX Composing DTP, Rayleigh, Essex
Printed and bound in Great Britain by Clays Ltd, Elcograf S.p.A.

www.methuen.co.uk

To Mia: Your love rescues my life

CONTENTS

PART FOUR: ACTION SUBGENRES

AUTHORS' NOTE

The *Action Genre* enacts the master metaphor for humanity's never-ending struggle of life versus death. Action sends a self-sacrificing hero against a self-obsessed villain in a story-long fight to thwart malevolence and rescue a hapless victim. These characters—hero, villain, victim—represent three opposing drives within every human being—the will to triumph, the impulse to destroy, and the hope to survive.

We wrote this book for you, the Action creative, to guide your exploration of this compelling genre and to inspire your finest work in its noble tradition.

INTRODUCTION

INTRODUCTION

In Part One: Action Cores, Chapter One outlines a twenty-first-century system for grouping stories by genre that divides all tellings into principal genres (differing contents) and presentational genres (differing forms of expression). Chapters Two through Five explore the core components of principal genres—core value, core cast, core event, core emotion—and how these four essentials inspire Action.

Part Two: Action Casts, Chapters Six and Seven, concentrates on the trio of forces that generate Action's inner energy: the hero/villain/victim complex.

Part Three: Action Designs, Chapters Eight through Sixteen, traces the shape of Action from inciting incident to climax.

Part Four: Action Subgenres, Chapters Seventeen through Twenty-Two, examines the genre's four subgenres, the four intra-subgenres inside each, and Action's most revered form: High Adventure. Part Four concludes with a call for originality.

A Note on Examples

We illustrate our chapters with examples that were popular when first shown or published, but more important, that illustrate the principles of the genre with precision and clarity. If you haven't seen them already, we recommend you familiarize yourself with *Die Hard*, *Mission: Impossible—Ghost Protocol*, *Terminator I–II*, *Back to the Future I–III*, *Men in Black I–III*, the *Star Wars* saga, *Guardians of the Galaxy*, *The Dark Knight*, *Casino Royale*, *The Matrix*, *Looper*, and *Avengers: Endgame*.

The Pronoun Problem

Some writers use the singular pronoun *he* as if it were unbiased, but *he* is not. On the other hand, the mind-stubbing word-jams of *s/he, he/she, her/him, he-and-she, her-and-him*, along with the pronoun *one* and the plural pronouns of *they, them*, and *their* used to neutralize gender, well intentioned as they are, slow the read. So, in odd-numbered chapters, unspecified persons will be female; in even-numbered chapters, they will be male.

PROLOGUE: THE LOVE OF ACTION

For tens of thousands of years, our nomadic ancestors celebrated their hand-to-hand, jaw-to-jaw, kill-or-be-killed adventures in firelit dance. As language evolved, epic poets (Homer the most famous) elaborated these mimed exploits into rhymed retellings hundreds of thousands of words long, memorized and recited verbatim. Decades later, scribes committed these massive oral performances to the written word, culminating in masterpieces such as *The Odyssey*, *The Iliad*, *The Mahabharata*, and *The Epic of Gilgamesh*.

Over the three millennia after Homer, a learned elite sustained the genre with works in both verse and prose such as *Beowulf*, *Njál's Saga*, *The Song of Nibelungs*, *The Song of Roland*, and *The Life of al-Zahir Baibars*. Finally, literacy, along with the motion picture, penetrated all echelons of society until Action became what it is today—the world's most popular storytelling genre.

Our love of Action begins when play becomes adventure. As we go from crawling on all fours to tottering on two to running from room to room, our imaginations transform climbing a flight of stairs into an assault on a fortress; bounding down, an escape from a monster. The living room rug becomes a battleground and toys become heroes and villains. Our imaginations rescue the blameless and punish the bad guys, instinctively acting out the eternal struggle between Good and Evil.

As we age, our love for Action matures, demanding greater and greater innovation. Year in, year out, excellent actioneers not only satisfy our wishes but express their visions with dazzling originality. Indeed, in the hands of the best action creators, the genre's conventions greet us like old friends born anew, changed yet unchanged.

Action, because of its popularity, has become one of the most demanding storytelling genres, originality its greatest challenge. In the last century alone, tens, perhaps hundreds of thousands of iterations have played out across page, screen, and game. Clichés litter its landscape. Like the prolific genres of Crime and Horror, the immense volume of Action writing has brought it to the saturation point.

How can today's author invent an Action sequence tomorrow's fans haven't seen or read ad infinitum in the past? How can the modern writer win the ancient war on clichés? How can you create not just a good Action Story but a great one? *Action: The Art of Excitement* illuminates this challenge and guides the writer to successful originality.

PART 1

ACTION CORES

1

THE MODERN GENRES

The multiplicity of life cannot be contained within a thousand stories, let alone one. From all the events that could ever happen, all the people an artist could ever imagine, all the values that preoccupy the mind, all the emotions that can be felt, writers must make choices of what to emphasize, what to excise. Over millennia of oral, enacted, written, and screened works, these choices have coalesced around the story types we call genres.

As readers and audiences enjoy and reenjoy their favorite genres, they develop an appetite for specific experiences and feel a loss when those pleasures go missing. Writers executing works in a particular genre naturally seek to satisfy these appetites with content and form that's familiar yet unique.

PRINCIPAL VS. **PRESENTATIONAL** GENRES

PRINCIPAL	**PRESENTATIONAL**
WHAT THE STORY IS ABOUT	**HOW THE STORY IS PRESENTED**
*Ground a story's **inner** components of core value, cast, event and emotion.*	*Express the content of a story **outwardly** in a particular style.*

Principal genres create content: events, characters, emotions, and values. Their telling turns the lives of characters positively or negatively, resulting in meaningful emotional experiences for audiences and readers.

These primal story types range from Crime Stories to Love Stories to Family Dramas to Action.

Presentational genres express content: They style the story as comic or dramatic, gritty or poetic, factual or fantasied, in a specific setting, for a specific length of performance time, on page, stage, or screen. These stylistic choices range from the Musical to the Documentary to Farce to Tragedy.

THE ORIGIN OF PRINCIPAL GENRES

The principal storytelling genres evolved in reaction to life's four essential levels of conflict: physical, social, personal, private.

Battles against the forces of nature—fire, flood, earthquakes, lightning, beasts—inspired storytellers to dramatize physical struggles. The most frequent threat to anyone's life, however, comes from other human beings, so storytellers also developed tales of social and personal clashes. These three levels—physical, social, personal—generate arcs of changing fortunes in a character's outer life. Change within a character's inner nature happens out of sight within the private realms of self-awareness and subconsciousness.

Few stories are so pure that their events take place on only one level of antagonism. Modern Action often mixes or merges with other primal forms, drawing on multiple sources of enmity. But to distinguish one story from another, let's look at how levels of conflict inspired the now familiar genres.

SELF VERSUS PHYSICAL FORCES

The Ancient Epic

Primeval adventure tales pit heroes against the powers of nature personified as gods: Odysseus battles a hurricane driven by the breath of Poseidon, Gilgamesh slaughters the Bull of Heaven, and thousands more.

The Horror Story

In addition to nature's personification as gods, the ancients also cast it as monsters such as the Hydra, Chimera, Minotaur, Cyclops, Mormo the vampire, Lycaon the werewolf, and Medusa the Gorgon—each a nightmare of imagination.

SELF VERSUS SOCIAL FORCES

The War Story

Tribe-on-tribe warfare grew into nation against nation, inspiring Homer's *Iliad*, his spectacle-in-verse depicting the Trojan War.

The Political Story

When the city-state of Athens instituted democracy in 508 BC, the power struggles that soon followed motivated the tragedies of Sophocles (*Antigone, Ajax, Philoctetes*) as well as the farces of Aristophanes (*The Wasps, The Clouds, The Frogs*).

The Crime Story

Crime detection first gained fame with Edgar Allan Poe's "The Murders in the Rue Morgue" (1841) and his investigative genius Auguste Dupin. Crime fiction went viral when Arthur Conan Doyle gave the world Sherlock Holmes.

The Modern Epic

Spurred by the rise of authoritarianism and its effacement of the individual, modern writers revamped the adventure tale into a fight for freedom that puts a lone hero up against an all-powerful tyrant. Underdog versus overdog tellings span both realism and nonrealism: *Spartacus, 1984, Braveheart, The Handmaid's Tale, Star Wars*.

The Social Drama

Upheavals in the nineteenth century exposed economic and political injustices as well as gender and racial inequalities. These stories identify social conflicts and dramatize their possible cures. The novelist Charles

Dickens and playwright Henrik Ibsen spent their literary lives exposing various inequities. Today, stories advocating social change have become a major cultural force.

The Enterprise Story

These tales track the struggle for success and threat of failure in the lives of professionals such as scientists, athletes, entrepreneurs, architects, or inventors.

SELF VERSUS PERSONAL RELATIONSHIPS

The various levels of intimate relationships create settings for personal conflicts within families and between friends or lovers.

The Family Story

From *Medea* to *King Lear* to *Succession*, family stories provide an unending source of inspiration. They dramatize the acts of loyalty and betrayal that bind together or drive apart parents and their children.

The Love Story

In the late Middle Ages, plagues of rape swept through Europe. To civilize male behavior, troubadours, the pop-culture artists of their day, idealized romance with songs and tales praising the virtues of chaste, chivalric love. Since then, waves of Romanticism followed by tides of anti-Romanticism have buoyed and swamped Western culture and the Love Stories it tells.

SELF VERSUS SELF RELATIONSHIPS

Tellings that arc a character's inner nature express how and why she changes her private self from who she is at the inciting incident to who she becomes by climax. What can an author change within a character's secret self? One of three possibilities: morality, mentality, humanity—each offering either a positive or a negative arc of change.

Morality: how a character treats other people—well or ill. *Mentality*: how a protagonist sees reality and herself within it—meaningful or meaningless. *Humanity*: how a protagonist's human potential changes—evolving to a fuller self or devolving to a lesser self.

These inner arcs offer authors six avenues of character change, three positive, three negative.*

Action Stories rarely arc the inner nature. They prefer to drive change along the physical, social, and personal levels. So, let's set hidden conflicts aside for a later chapter and examine ten principal modern genres that dramatize change in a cast's outer fortunes. As you read the list below, notice how the simple story types that were originally inspired by life's levels of conflict have evolved into complex forms. Note also how Action compares and overlaps with the other nine principal genres.

TWENTY-FIRST-CENTURY GENRES OF OUTER CHANGE

Each principal genre contains four essential conventions: core value, core cast, core event, and core emotion.

THE **CORE CONVENTIONS** OF GENRE

1. CORE **VALUE**
2. CORE **CAST**
3. CORE **EVENT**
4. CORE **EMOTION**

By *value* we mean a duality of positive versus negative: Life/Death,

---

* For more on the six genres that arc the inner life, see Chapter Ten: The Complex Character in *Character: The Art of Role and Cast Design for Page, Stage, and Screen* by Robert McKee.

Love/Hate, Good/Evil, Victory/Defeat, Justice/Injustice, Freedom/Slavery, Truth/Lie, and many others.

STORY VALUE

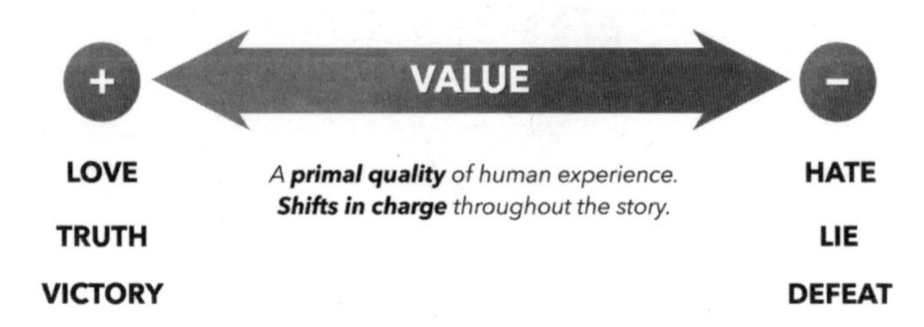

By *core* we mean a value so indispensable to the telling that without it a story becomes an empty recitation of "... and then and then and then ..." Each principal genre takes one of these binaries as its essential source of meaning and energy.

CORE VALUE

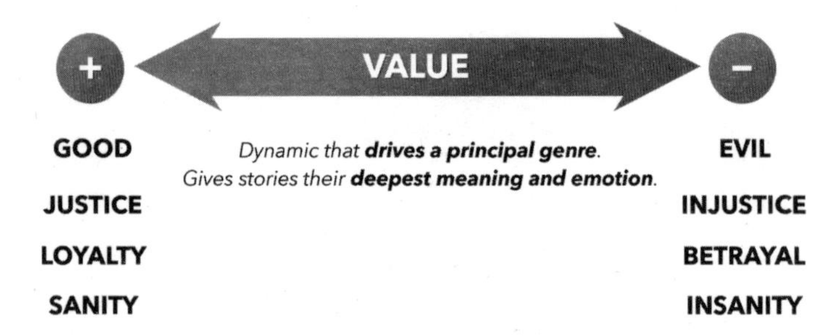

By *core cast* we mean the genre's essential roles.

By *core event* we mean the genre's critical turning point. Without this pivotal scene, the plot's chain of events breaks, rendering the story pointless or dull.

By *core emotion* we mean the unique experience the genre engenders in an audience or reader.

In this section we will discuss the ten principal genres that arc the

THE **CORE CAST** OF THE **CRIME GENRE**

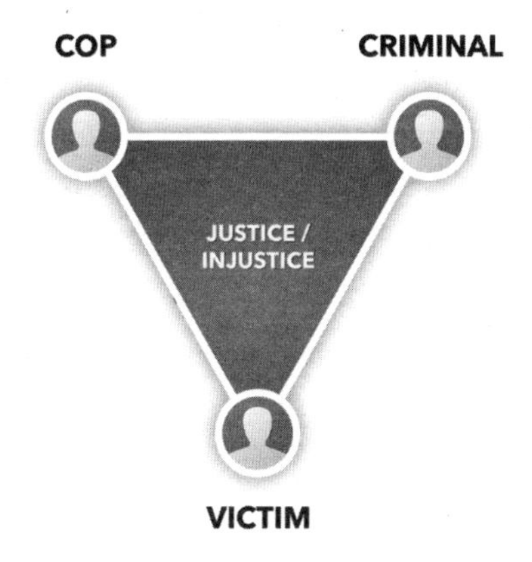

THE **CORE CAST** OF THE **LOVE GENRE**

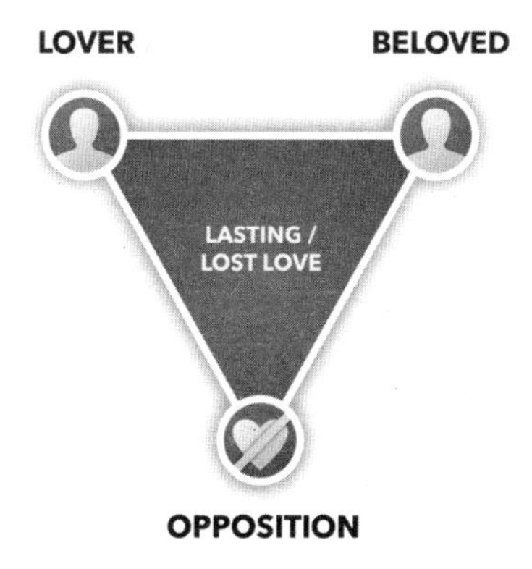

THE **CORE CAST** OF THE **WAR GENRE**

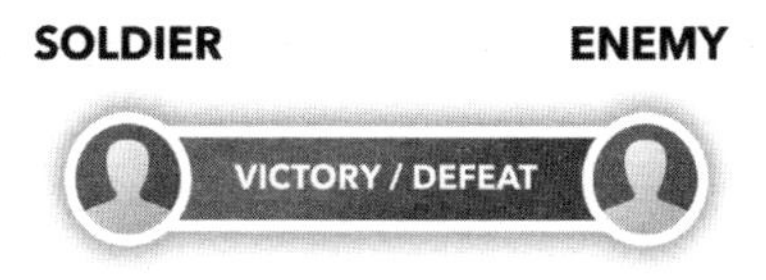

outer lives of their characters and the quartet of core conventions for each. As we will see in later chapters, these genres often mix and merge with Action, but for now we'll look at them individually.

1. The Crime Genre

CORE VALUE: JUSTICE VERSUS INJUSTICE
CORE CAST: COP, CRIMINAL, VICTIM
CORE EVENT: EXPOSURE OF THE CRIMINAL
CORE EMOTION: SUSPENSE

Over the past two centuries, the Crime Genre protagonist has evolved from an ingenious, cool-minded investigator with hard-edged morality to a psychologically and emotionally complex guy or gal with flexible ethics. (See the series *Mare of Easttown*.)

2. The War Genre

CORE VALUE: VICTORY VERSUS DEFEAT
CORE CAST: SOLDIER, ENEMY
CORE EVENT: THE DECISIVE BATTLE
CORE EMOTION: HARROWING FEAR

A successful military strategy hinges on the courage to carry it out. This genre calls for characters who act despite fear. (See *Fury*.)

3. The Epic Genre

CORE VALUE: TYRANNY VERSUS FREEDOM
CORE CAST: TYRANT, REBEL
CORE EVENT: AN ACT OF REBELLION
CORE EMOTION: MORAL OUTRAGE

The protagonists of this genre battle tyranny. In Fantasy Epics—*The Hunger Games, Star Wars, Game of Thrones*—tyrants never survive. In Historical Epics—*Spartacus, Braveheart, The Good Lord Bird*—protagonists never survive.

4. The Political Genre

CORE VALUE: POWER VERSUS WEAKNESS
CORE CAST: TWO COMBATIVE PARTIES
CORE EVENT: POWER WON OR LOST
CORE EMOTION: HUNGER FOR VICTORY

As political adversaries battle for power, their partisan beliefs become virtually irrelevant. In political warfare, the weapon of mass destruction is scandal: bribes, backstabbings, and, above all, illicit sex. Stories of conflicts between criminal gangs often have little to do with crime but much in common with politics. (See *Godfather of Harlem*.)

A telling may begin in what looks like a setup for a Crime, War, Epic, or Political Drama, but then evolve into Action as protagonist and antagonist turn into hero and villain.

5. The Horror Genre

CORE VALUE: SURVIVAL VERSUS DAMNATION
CORE CAST: MONSTER, VICTIM
CORE EVENT: VICTIM AT THE MERCY OF THE MONSTER
CORE EMOTION: IRRATIONAL TERROR

Horror eliminates the Action hero to focus on the monster/victim conflict. The Action Genre inspires excitement; Horror provokes terror. Action keeps the reader and audience at a safe emotional distance; Horror assaults the subconscious. Think of Action as a force, Horror as an invasion.

Action villains obey the laws of nature; monsters either break these laws with supernatural power or bend them with power of an uncanny magnitude. An Action villain is a narcissist; the Horror monster is a sadist. The villain possesses the spirit of narcissism; the fiend possesses the spirit of evil. Wealth, power, and fame will satisfy a villain's vanity, but the monster inflicts pain and prolongs suffering because the agony of his victim gives him sublime pleasure. (See *A Nightmare on Elm Street*.)

6. The Social Genre

CORE VALUE: PROBLEM VERSUS SOLUTION
CORE CAST: SOCIAL LEADER, VICTIM
CORE EVENT: THE PROBLEM REACHES CRISIS
CORE EMOTION: MORAL INDIGNATION

The Social Genre identifies problems such as poverty, racism, genderism, and child abuse and then dramatizes the protagonists' search for a solution. (See *BlackkKlansman*.)

7. The Enterprise Genre

CORE VALUE: SUCCESS VERSUS FAILURE
CORE CAST: PROTAGONIST, SOCIAL INSTITUTION
CORE EVENT: A PROFESSIONAL LOSS
CORE EMOTION: ROOTING FOR SUCCESS

An ambitious protagonist—entrepreneur, athlete, scientist—strives to achieve her ambition. (See *Ford v Ferrari*.)

8. The Love Genre

CORE VALUE: LASTING VERSUS LOST LOVE
CORE CAST: LOVERS
CORE EVENT: AN ACT OF LOVE
CORE EMOTION: LONGING FOR LOVE

Romantic rituals, no matter how deeply felt, are simply gestures of affection. The only act of genuine love is an anonymous self-sacrifice—a silent deed taken without hope of recognition or reward that benefits the beloved but costs the lover dearly. If love does not hurt, it is not real. The final test of a Love Story is the creation of an act of love that is unique to your characters and deeply moving to your reader/audience.

In many Action films, from *Raiders of the Lost Ark* to *Allied*, a Love Story adds a subplot.

9. The Domestic Genre

CORE VALUE: UNITY VERSUS BREAKUP
CORE CAST: A FAMILY
CORE EVENT: A CRISIS OF DEVOTION
CORE EMOTION: LONGING FOR TOGETHERNESS

The cast of a Domestic Drama may or may not be blood relatives, but no matter how the group was formed, its members, even if they don't love one another, commit to mutual unity as they struggle to stay together. (See *The Incredibles II*.)

10. The Action Genre

CORE VALUE: LIFE VERSUS DEATH
CORE CAST: HERO, VILLAIN, VICTIM
CORE EVENT: HERO AT THE MERCY OF THE VILLAIN
CORE EMOTION: EXCITEMENT

THE **CORE CONVENTIONS** OF ACTION

1. CORE **VALUE**: *Life vs. Death*
2. CORE **CAST**: *Hero, Villain, Victim*
3. CORE **EVENT**: *Hero at the Mercy of the Villain*
4. CORE **EMOTION**: *Excitement*

The core cast of Action forms a triangle of moral archetypes. The essential trait of the hero is altruism; of the villain, narcissism; of the victim, vulnerability.

Each of these ten genres envelops subgenres: Crime, for example, has fourteen; Love, six; Action, four. We will explore the subgenres of Action and their sixteen intra-subgenres in Part Four.

GENRE COMBINATIONS

When a central plot in one genre intercuts with a subplot in another, the contrast expands character complexity. In a typical example, if an Action Genre central plot splices with a Love Story subplot, the telling pulls the protagonist back and forth between the tough qualities called for in Action and the light touches needed in Romance. (See *Romancing the Stone*.)

PRESENTATIONAL GENRES

Once a writer chooses her principal genre and shapes a telling within it, she must give these events a voice. Presentational genres focus her choices of expression: Which medium best conveys her story: Screen? Page? Stage? In what setting should it take place? What stylistics best express its visual and auditory mood? How long the telling? At what pace? Where in time: Present? Past? Future? Below are ten presentational choices. Each of these possibilities, even the Musical, could express an Action tale.

PRESENTATIONAL GENRES

1. TONAL
2. MUSICAL
3. SCIENCE-FICTION
4. HISTORY
5. ONTOLOGY
6. DOCUMENTARY
7. ANIMATION
8. AUTOBIOGRAPHY
9. BIOGRAPHY
10. HIGH ART

1. Tonal

A spectrum of tone runs from Tragedy to Farce, from the solemn to the satirical. Any principal genre could first treat life seriously, then flip to a lighter tone, then move back into the darkness. Or reverse that dynamic: a swing from comedy to drama and back to comedy.

2. Musical

Any principal genre could be sung and danced.

3. Science-Fiction

Any genre could be set in a futuristic world or a tech-driven present or past.

4. History

Any genre could take place in a previous era.

5. Ontology

Ontology means the nature of a story's reality. Any genre could take place in a naturalistic setting or in one of the nonrealisms that range from magical to fantasied to supernatural to the absurd.

6. Documentary

Any genre could be told factually.

7. Animation

Any genre could be animated.

8. Autobiography

Any genre could dramatize a memoir.

9. Biography

Any genre could dramatize a person's life.

10. High Art

Any story could be styled as cinematic art, avant-garde theatre, or literary fiction. In the Action Genre, High Art becomes High Adventure (as we will see in Chapter Twenty-Two).

To be clear, genres are the underlying forms that give stories substance and surface. A writer chooses among genres the way a composer chooses among classical, jazz, rock, or hip-hop, then among a solo voice or an instrument or ensemble or orchestra to best intone her melody. For the writer, the questions become: Which principal genre best embodies my vision? Which presentational genre best expresses it?

GENRE EVOLUTION

Cultures evolve slowly over time, and as they do, their storytelling transforms as well. Authors, therefore, like antennae attuned to the world around them, bend or break genre conventions to fit the changing perceptions of their audiences and readers. Writers adapt principal genres to changing cultural and political forces. They retune presentational genres by repurposing innovations like the internet. The evolution of the female hero, for one example, is a major advance. As a result, the Action Stories we're telling now are light-years beyond stories told just a decade ago.

Once you master the structures and techniques of Action, you are free to use, change, or ignore its conventions in whichever way you see fit. Action offers you any setting, any medium, any length, any voice. The most important creative choices are always yours.

The next four chapters put these choices to work as we examine the four foundational components of Action: core cast, core value, core emotion, and core event.

2

THE CORE VALUE OF ACTION

Of the four core aspects that compose a principal genre (cast, action, emotion, value), value is the feature that clearly defines each and sets it apart. Core value not only determines a genre's subject matter and shapes its meaning but also electrifies its telling with energy.

Story values are living contradictions of a positive versus negative charge such as Truth/Lie, Love/Hate, Freedom/Slavery. A story could infuse its events with a dynamic moral paradox (Good/Evil), a social dilemma (Justice/Injustice), a personal clash (Loyalty/Betrayal), or a warring inner state (Sanity/Insanity). Over the course of any story, a core binary value powers the deepest emotions. As this value shifts its charge from positive to negative, negative to positive, characters win and lose, suffer and survive, propelling events to climax.

If an audience/reader cannot sense a value pulsating through the characters' lives, interest muddles into confusion and emotions dissolve into indifference. Without a core value, events make no sense, characters stir no emotion.

The core value in the Action Genre is Life/Death.

This dynamic has inspired every Action tale from *The Epic of Gilgamesh* (2000 BC) to *No Time to Die* (AD 2021). Action dramas such as *The Odyssey*, *Moby-Dick*, *Die Hard*, and *Star Wars* as well as Action comedies such as *Guardians of the Galaxy*, *Kung Fu Hustle*, and *Men in Black* share this same core value. Throughout the whole of history, Action tales from every culture, infinite in nuance and variety, have pulsed with the struggle to take one more breath.

THE **CORE VALUE** OF ACTION

The dynamic ***struggle to exist,***

Stories in the Crime Genre turn on the legal consequences of injustice; tales of redemption arc a protagonist from immoral to moral. The Action Genre, however, ignores both legality and morality. Instead, it keeps the traits of hero and villain vividly polarized. Heroes, even if they break the law, remain heroic; villains, even if they're loyal to each other, remain villainous. This moral dichotomy allows the Action writer to focus on what excites the most: the imminence of death.

Life/Death gives Action its essential meaning. Unless extinction is at stake, excitement melts into boredom. Without the threat of death, an Action Story, no matter how violent, becomes empty choreography.

The variety and subtlety of positive/negative charges in Action's core value span myriad emotional experiences from adrenaline surges of euphoria to grief over a lost loved one. So, although subplots often bring other values into play, Life/Death offers enough diversity of conflict to carry a full-length work on its own.

3

THE CORE CAST OF ACTION

The principal genres cast a minimum number of specific roles to execute the necessary events.

In the ideal cast, no two characters share the same attitude toward people around them or even life itself. Instead, their natures contrast with, or even contradict, each other. As a result, no two characters take the same actions and no two react the same to anything that happens. Each role performs its specific tasks in its specific way.

Here are three familiar examples:

Love Stories cast three core roles: lover, beloved, and an antagonistic force opposed to love. Once the lover and beloved meet, their intimacy builds toward a lifetime of commitment. At some point, however, an adverse force enters the telling to test the lovers' fidelity. This third role comes in an unlimited variety of forms, from an opposing family, society, race, or religion to a rival lover. A negative force might also arise from within the lovers themselves, pitting psychological or emotional incompatibilities against one another. Conflicting political allegiances in *Lust, Caution*, for instance, not only destroy the lovers' affair but end their lives as well.

The Crime Genre anchors in a core cast of cop, crook, society. A cop investigates a crime, trying to identify, apprehend, and punish a criminal, and thus win justice for society.

War Stories need just two core roles: warrior versus enemy. The two battle toward final victory or defeat as each risks her life to win the war for her side. For example: In *Hell in the Pacific*, a downed American pilot and a stranded Japanese soldier fight to the death on an uninhabited island.

THE ACTION GENRE

The Action Genre casts three core roles: hero, villain, victim.

THE **CORE CAST** OF THE **ACTION GENRE**

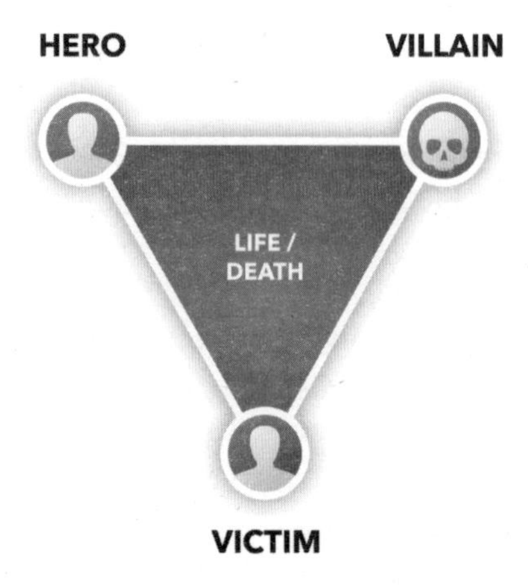

This triad shapes the Action Story as villains endanger victims that heroes must save. Each of these characters projects a unique spirit that not only defines herself but contrasts her relationship with the other two.

HEROISM: THE SPIRIT OF ALTRUISM

The shades of power in a hero run from superhero (Superman) to action hero (Lara Croft) to everyman hero (Captain Phillips). Superheroes employ extra-human powers to battle extra-human villains; action heroes test their strengths against conventional villains; everyday heroes have no special skills, except the will to endure.

RANGE OF **HEROES**

In classically told stories, the protagonist propels events to closure, a final turning point beyond which the audience or reader cannot and does not imagine another. This climax tests the lead role to the limits of her human potential. In the Action Genre, the central character must do all this and be fully heroic as well.

The term *hero* implies more than courage or fighting skills. We admire a surgeon's steady nerves as she saves a life on an operating table or a social worker's compassion as she saves a child from drug addiction. But in these cases, the professional's personal life keeps its distance from the patient's or client's life. In an act of true heroism, however, two lives connect: One person sacrifices her life to save the life of another.

In a high-tension genre such as Horror, a protagonist fights to save her life from a hideous death . . . but only her life and no one else's. When Horror audiences and readers identify with a victim in terrifying jeopardy, they often feel the tremulous emotions of terror and dread.

HEROISM: THE SPIRIT OF **ALTRUISM**

*Entails more than **courage** or **fighting skill**.*
*Heroes exhibit the instinct for **self-sacrifice**: **risking their lives** to **save others**.*
*The audience **empathizes** with the hero.*

When an Action Story hero rescues a victim from lethal danger, her act arouses excitement in the audience as the spirit of altruism carries her to the far end of the courage spectrum. She risks and, if necessary, erases her own existence to save the life of an innocent. The instinct for self-sacrifice places the hero at the story's center of good.

THE CENTER OF GOOD

We want to vicariously experience fictional events as if they were happening to us. But to do so, we must search through the traits and qualities of a story's cast and sort good from bad, positive from negative. We want to embroil ourselves, not just intellectually but personally. The moment our instincts spot a positive spark emanating from within a character, we instinctively connect with that kindred spirit, empathetically identify with the character, and immerse ourselves in her life. This role becomes the story's center of good.

We instinctively connect to the *good* because each of us feels that we, too, are essentially good. We know we're flawed, struggling to do better, but deep inside we feel that our heart is in the right place. When a story anchors a positive quality in its protagonist, and then surrounds this character with roles of lesser, dimmer, darker, even negative quality, the glowing light from within her draws our empathy and spurs emotional involvement. Once linked, we feel free to suffer or celebrate as if what happens to the protagonist were happening to us.

The moment a storygoer steps into a fictional world, she begins to inspect its value-charged universe, sorting positives from negatives, rights from wrongs, goods from evils, searching for a secure place to invest her empathy.

A story's center of good places a positive charge of value (Justice, Goodness, Love) deep within the telling, in clear contrast with the negative charges (Tyranny, Evil, Hate) that surround it. Human beings naturally identify with the positive rather than the negative because they feel that deep within themselves, despite their flaws, their essential nature is positive. As a result, readers and audiences instinctively project empathy toward their perception of an affirmative quality.

In Action, the center of good anchors in the hero's altruism. Her self-sacrificing nature keeps her personal misery, no matter how bloodied, at a safe emotional distance from readers and audiences, allowing them to identify with her moral strength. As a result, the knife-edge of danger in the Action Genre inspires high excitement but never descends into the intense fear of the Thriller, let alone the terror of Horror.

For instance: In *Terminator 2: Judgment Day*, the villainous T-1000 blasts the limbs and flesh off the heroic T-800, his severed wiring thrashing and crackling. The T-800 ultimately sacrifices himself in a vat of molten metal. But rather than making the audience recoil, his suffering and martyrdom arouse great excitement.

THE HEROIC ARC

The inner natures of heroes rarely change. Instead, the events that drive an Action Story pivot its hero's outer circumstances. The threat of death at the beginning (negative) arcs to either life (positive) or death (tragically negative) at climax. The hero's action choices under the threat of death reveal her inner nature but do not change it. By a story's climax, its hero has been revealed as essentially the same person she was when the story began, but now we have insight into who, beneath the surface, she really is—exactly how skillful, how determined, how intelligent, how altruistic.

HEROISM IN MIXED AND MERGED GENRES

Genres mix when story lines of different genres crosscut. If an Action central plot alternates with a subplot from another genre, the hero needs additional character traits, making her more complex.

A common mix of genres intercuts Action with subplots of the Buddy and Crime Genres: *Men in Black, Lethal Weapon, Rush Hour.* To the protagonist's core of heroic altruism, these admixtures stir in the wit and selflessness necessary for friendship plus the analytical skills of a detective.

Genres merge when a story line in one genre drives the outcome of another. If, for example, an Action Story merges with one of the six genres of character change, then as the hero tries to complete her mission, her morality, mentality, or humanity changes for better or worse.

Wreck-It Ralph, for instance, arcs the protagonist's morality from bad guy to good guy. In it, Ralph, a video game character, loathes his life as the villain in the very popular *Fix-It Felix*. His sole purpose in life is to play the hulking oaf that the hero, Fix-It Felix, beats every day, every game. Depressed, Ralph goes to a self-help group populated by video game villains who chant, "I'm bad and that's good. I will never be good and that's not bad." Ralph rejects their mantra and instead quests after a heroic role in another video game.

In this game, Ralph encounters a character whose life is in danger and makes an instinctive crisis decision to forfeit his life to save hers. With that, he reaches the height of altruism: sacrifice without reward. Ralph arcs a Redemption Plot from reluctant villain to altruistic hero.*

Guardians of the Galaxy takes merging genres a step further by combining Action with both the Redemption Genre and the Buddy Story (a subgenre of the Love Story). Its protagonists change from immoral criminals to heroic friends, each willing to die to save the other.

(The mentor, by the way, is not an Action role. The casts of *Die Hard*, *Jaws*, and *Guardians of the Galaxy* have no mentors, no guides. Mentors often play a supporting role in the Maturation Plot, one of the subgenres of the Evolution Genre. If an Action Plot merges with a coming-of-age story, then the protagonist may indeed need a mentor, as Rey needed Luke Skywalker and Yoda in the *Star Wars* saga.)

When you mix or merge genres, the growing complex of character traits tends to favor one facet of a hero's nature over another. So, which side is the most important? Is your protagonist a romantic hero or a heroic romantic? These are two different people. How you balance story lines guides you to which aspects dominate, which support, and how they interact.

VILLAINY: THE SPIRIT OF NARCISSISM

Villains range from supervillains to master criminals to street gangs.

They use violence without hesitation because they're indifferent to the humanity of their victims. The hero, in contrast, has to be provoked to violence because she cannot be indifferent to anyone's humanity,

---

* For more on the six genres of character change—Redemption, Degeneration, Education, Disillusionment, Evolution, Devolution—see Chapter Fourteen in *Character: The Art of Role and Cast Design for Page, Stage, and Screen* by Robert McKee.)

including the villain's. To the villain, heroes and victims are objects—a means to an end; to the hero, no one, not even the villain, is an object.

The full spectrum of villainy runs from bully to criminality to monstrosity.

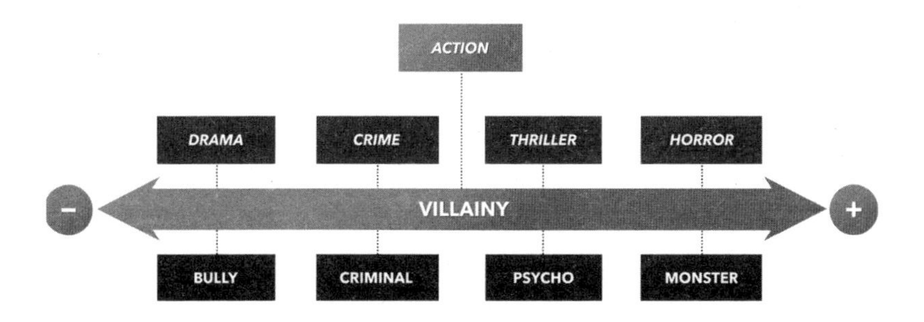

In the Crime Genre, criminals commit crimes and then avoid exposure. With success, they slip back into the normal world. In theory, therefore, criminals can be bought off. If society gave them enough riches, they would no longer bother to steal and kill.

In a Thriller, the villain often twists into a psychopathic personality that cannot be bought off. Trapped within her delusions, the psychopath ignores wealth. She measures pleasure in integers of the pain she causes.

At the furthest end of this spectrum waits the monster hidden in the

Horror Genre. This creature has no delusions. Its evil is clear-minded and pure. The criminal inflicts suffering on her victims; the psychopath inflicts a nightmare; the monster is the nightmare. Action villains sit somewhere along the criminal/psychopath/monster spectrum.

The *Diagnostic and Statistical Manual of Mental Disorders* (5th edition) describes sociopaths as "*. . . arrogant and self-centered, feeling privileged and entitled. They have a grandiose, exaggerated sense of self-importance and are primarily motivated by self-serving goals. They seek power over others and will manipulate, exploit, deceive, con, or otherwise take advantage of others. They are callous and have little empathy for others' needs and feelings unless they coincide with their own. They also have the capacity for superficial charm and ingratiation when it suits their purposes.*" This tracks villainy from the Big Bad Wolf in Little Red Riding Hood to Thanos in *Avengers: Endgame.*

The psychopathology of the Action villain inspires delusions of grandeur—a world and everyone in it on their knee to serve her. Heroes sacrifice themselves for others; villains sacrifice others for themselves.

But the Action Genre sets limits. The victims of an Action villain beg to live. That's a natural impulse. The victims of a Horror monster beg to die. That's an unnatural but credible reaction to the power of evil. The tortures inflicted by the monster in Horror make going out of existence seem merciful. Not only does the monster perpetrate hideous harm, but it then sits back to enjoy its victim's suffering.

VILLAINY: THE SPIRIT OF **NARCISSISM**

VILLAINY

Villains exhibit the capacity to ***sacrifice others for themselves****.*
The ***vanity*** *of the villain counterpoints the* ***altruism*** *of the hero.*
Often display ***delusions of grandeur****.*
The audience feels ***antipathy*** *for the villain.*

The spirit of a monster is sadism, but in Action, the villain's narcissistic core drives the telling. She may take a moment's pleasure in the suffering she causes, may even seem irrational or repulsive in some sense, but at heart she is in love with herself. Everything revolves around her and her plan.

Unlike criminals in Crime Stories, the Action villain cannot be bought off. She has a scheme that defines her life, a perfect project that's greater than herself. This stratagem is both opaque and mysterious (otherwise it's just lawbreaking) and extremely disruptive (otherwise ordinary cops could handle it).

The villain's pursuit of her desire and the execution of her plan to reach it necessitate her creation of victims: hostages on a hijacked plane, civilians under a bombing strike, the afflicted swept up in a man-made plague. Whatever the villain hopes to achieve, someone else must pay the price, and from the villain's point of view, why not? The villain feels she's smarter than the hero and her cause more righteous than her victims' lives. Who dare stand in her way?

Villains often justify their villainy with an appeal to a higher moral cause as they picture themselves as righteous martyrs or victims fighting social injustice. But we know a role's true character by the choices she makes under the pressure of life. Villains expose their villainy when they consistently choose self over others, justifying their deeds with the thought: "What I want is essential. To get it, other people are expendable."

To sum up: The villain's vanity counterpoints the hero's altruism and sets up their dynamic, polarized morality. The writer tasks the villain with endangering lives, the victim with the inability to save herself, and the hero with the necessity of defeating the villain and rescuing the victim. Together, hero/villain/victim forge the triangle of relationships that inspire Action.

VICTIMHOOD: THE SPIRIT OF HELPLESSNESS

The vulnerable victim comes in many personae: child, lover, family, small town, nation, planet Earth, even the universe. Victims are essential. Without them, heroes cannot be heroic, nor villains villainous. A well-characterized, well-realized victim is as indispensable to Action as hero and villain.

Helplessness, fully dramatized, is foundational to the Action Genre. If a victim fights back and wins, what becomes of a villain's menace? If a victim saves herself, what role does a hero play? But when a writer's insights into the psychology of victimhood express helplessness at its most complex, villains become fascinatingly villainous, heroes stunningly heroic, and the genre thrives.

VICTIMHOOD: THE SPIRIT OF **HELPLESSNESS**

VICTIMHOOD

Victims possess the ***inability to save themselves****.*
Vulnerable *but not necessarily* ***cowardly****.*
The audience feels ***sympathy*** *for the victim.*

The spirit of helplessness does not call for cowardice in a victim; it simply means she cannot save herself. A brave child may persistently resist the villain but lack the physical capacity to escape for whatever original, insightful reason you can invent. Just as a hero's altruistic spirit draws empathy from the audience/reader, a victim's well-dramatized helplessness draws sympathy. The difference is this: We empathize, indeed identify, with heroes, seeing ourselves in them, thinking the thought: "That hero is like me. Therefore, if I were in the hero's situation, I would do what the hero does." But we do not identify with victims. Rather than "like me," a victim seems "likable" or sympathetic. We now think this thought: "That victim is vulnerable. If I were there, I would try to save her. She needs me." Heroes draw empathy; victims draw sympathy; villains draw antipathy.

4

THE CORE EVENT OF ACTION

A genre's core event distills its essence. This major turning point expresses both the genre's core value at its most dynamic and its core emotion at its most intense. What's more, it answers key questions of character: Who hides in the depths of this cast? Who of them is moral? Who immoral? Weak or willful? Courageous or cowardly? Clever or foolish? Impulsive or cool?

The core event plays off all prior setups and sets up all subsequent events. It may be a story's inciting incident, such as the rebellion that launches a Modern Epic, or the story's climax, such as the battle that ends a War Story. The Crime Genre pivots around the exposure of the criminal, a turning point that may come early or late in the telling. A criminal may ultimately get away with his crime, as does Frank Sheeran in *The Irishman*, but he can't go unidentified. A whodunnit that doesn't reveal whodunnit is itself a crime.

THE MERCY SCENE

An Action telling coils into extreme tension the instant it traps the hero at the mercy of the villain. The mercy scene posits the weaponless protagonist at his weakest and the weapon-rich antagonist at his most powerful, and then calls for the hero to somehow turn tables on the villain and come out on top.

THE **CORE EVENT** OF ACTION

This scene can pause to take all the time it needs as it fills up on high-tension fuel. Until now, the hero has prevented the villain from killing him, but in this frozen moment, the defenseless, back-to-the-wall hero stares up into the villain's triumphant smile—all seems lost.

The mercy scene raises this question: Why doesn't the villain just kill the hero when he has the chance? The answer exploits a weakness in the villain: narcissism. Vanity drives the villain to gloat over the hapless hero, to revel in joyful triumph and perhaps torture him for information or sadistic pleasure.

Tension tightens as the torment builds. At its peak, the mercy scene pushes conflict to a nail-biting brink as the villain sights his weapon, poised to take the final, fatal step and execute the hero. How can a hero, from one moment to the next, pivot from victim to victorious? In one of three ways: He can overpower or outsmart or do both at once.

To overpower the villain, the hero must master the villain's strength and then use that leverage to surpass him, might against might. Martial arts films call on this technique almost exclusively. Chinese literature, however, features many masterpieces of Action such as the *Legends of Condor Heroes*. Author Jing Yong mixes and merges heroic tales with genres of War, Politics, Love, and the Evolution Plot. His protagonists defeat villains with both martial skill and psychological insight.

To outsmart the villain, the hero must discover a weakness in the villain and then exploit that flaw to defeat him. In many cases, the villain's excess power or unstoppable momentum becomes a weakness, and in a judo-like move, the hero flips jeopardy into triumph. One of their most common flaws is arrogance. When victory goes to a villain's head, he's suddenly distractible and vulnerable.

In the mercy scene in *Die Hard*, the hero both outsmarts and overpowers the villain. First, outsmarting: John McClane, the blood-smeared, hands-in-the-air defeated hero, improvises an ingenious solution: He distracts the villains, Hans Gruber and his henchman Eddie, by suddenly scoffing at the absurdity of their showdown. Second, when the villains get the joke and crack up laughing, McClane overpowers them by grabbing a gun he secretly taped to his back, killing Eddie, and wounding Hans. Hero and villain then fight hand-to-hand until McClane drops Hans from the thirtieth floor of Nakatomi Plaza.

MERCY SCENE SETUPS

Heroes often enter a story with multiple resources. To reach a state of helplessness, events must strip the hero of his weapons and sidekicks until he's defenseless and alone. In essence, all early demonstrations of the hero's powers make their step-by-step loss more and more impactful, deepening into a crisis. As the hero's abilities disappear, the villain's powers grow proportionately, building to the final mercy scene face-off.

PLACEMENT

Because the mercy scene expresses all four core conventions of Action—value (Life/Death), emotion (excitement), cast (hero/villain/victim), and event—at their peaks in one turning point, the writer's natural tendency is to save the best for last and use it to climax the story, as did *Die Hard*. But not necessarily . . .

The mercy scene could cap the penultimate act to set up the final climax (*Skyfall*); it could start the story by opening as the inciting incident and then become a vastly complicated action that fills the entire story from start to finish (*The Raid*); it's even possible, although exceedingly rare, that the hero fails to turn tables and the antagonist triumphs (*The Perfect Storm*). Use your mercy scene in whatever way seems truest to your world and characters.

FAILED MERCY SCENES

Storygoers love the core event in their favorite genre. If a telling deletes this scene or its performance seems unconvincing, audiences and readers react as if robbed at gunpoint. They may not know exactly why they're disappointed, but they know failure when they feel it.

THE **CORE EVENT** OF ACTION

FAILED MERCY SCENE

- X **ABSENT VILLAIN**
- X **ACHILLES' HEEL**
- X **CLICHÉD DISTRACTION**
- X **COINCIDENCE**
- X **LAST-MINUTE RESCUE**

The mercy scene is the single most difficult code to crack in all of Action writing. It calls for brilliant creative ingenuity. As a result, the history of Action is littered with letdowns. Here's a short list of failed choices:

1. Absent Villains

Henchmen are notoriously easy to outsmart and overcome (see the *John Wick* franchise). Leaving the execution of the hero to a goon makes table turning as easy as a card trick. As a result, these mercy scenes fall flat, leaving readers and audiences to wonder, "If this isn't important enough for the villain to be here, why should I care?"

The deep purpose of the mercy scene is to express the hero's ingenious cool under pressure in contradiction to the villain's egomaniacal blindness. To pull this off, we put hero and villain face-to-face—if not physically, at least electronically.

2. Achilles' Heels

If a writer cannot outsmart his own villain, he often plants an obvious flaw or weakness in the character, a string to pull to turn the core event. The veteran storygoer, of course, can see an Achilles' heel coming long before the mercy scene puts it in play and so suffers the "I saw it coming" blues.

3. Clichéd Distractions

Outsmarting by distraction is an ancient device, encrusted with clichés such as "Look out, there's someone behind you," and "Uh-oh, your shoelace is untied." Avoid them.

4. Coincidences

The same is true for bits of random good luck, such as a car backfiring in the street outside that makes the villain think he's under attack and then flee the mercy scene.

5. Last-Minute Rescues

The Latin phrase *deus ex machina* names the plot device that originated in the theaters of Athens and Rome beginning twenty-five hundred years ago. When classical playwrights couldn't find an ending, they would call for a god to suddenly enter the play and solve the protagonist's problems. The actor playing this all-powerful deity stood on an elevated platform and, as if descending from heaven, was lowered to the stage by a pulley system of ropes—a machine. Hence, *deus ex machina*, which translates as "god from machine."

In modern writing, *deus ex machina* involves the use of a lame, extraneous cause to get the writer out of his plot. Hack action doesn't use a literal god to rescue its hero but various substitutes: *deus ex partner, deus ex lover, deus ex cops, deus ex luck, deus ex traitor from within the villain's crew.*

Any shortcut that takes critical decisions and actions out of the hero's or villain's hands cripples an Action Story and deprives audiences and readers of excitement, the genre's core emotion.

5

THE CORE EMOTION OF ACTION

Emotion is the side effect of change. So long as the values governing a person's life balance—her successes offset her failures, her sense of safety calms her sense of danger—she goes about her days coolly and rationally. But when a life value suddenly changes and swings out of balance, emotion floods her being. If her professional life, for example, pivots from negative to positive (a project moves from problem to solution), feel-good hormones such as dopamine and serotonin lift her spirits. If a personal relationship reverses from positive to negative (a close friend betrays her), she suffers an outpouring of disruptive hormones, prompting emotions such as rage, fear, or sadness.

EMOTION AND MEANING

In life, emotion and meaning come separately, first one, then the other. When an unexpected event throws life out of balance, emotion rushes through us. As things quiet down, we think about why this happened and what caused the change.

Suppose an old friend suddenly insults us and ends the relationship. Shock and hurt cause days and weeks of wondering what went wrong and what, if anything, we did to cause it.

Over time, our ruminations add to our knowledge of life. When a similar event occurs in the future, our emotional reaction is less disruptive, our sense of what to do more astute. We have learned something about people and ourself. In other words, life experience follows this pattern: first an emotional reaction, then an effort to make sense.

Fiction tells a different tale. Unlike the raw, often confusing jolts of life and the struggle over time to find meaning, when a story's turning point surprises us, a flash of insight suddenly floods our mind as we instantly glimpse the hidden cause buried in the previous events that triggered what just happened. In the same moment that we catch sight of these hows and whys, a flood of emotional energy, positive or negative, engulfs our feelings.

The moment Obadiah Stane betrays Tony Stark in *Iron Man*, the audience's mind rushes back through the film's setups and instantly grasps Stane's ruthless greed for power.

This fusion of meaning and emotion marks the grand difference between aesthetic experience and daily life. When we listen to a superb piece of music or gaze on a wondrous sculpture, the two sides of our nature—thought and feeling—simultaneously link within us, touching depths and shaping qualities that the everyday denies. Works of art unify the two realms life separates: the rational and the emotional. Simply put, art charges meaning with feeling.

EMPATHY VERSUS DISTANCE

For the storyteller, meaningful emotion hinges on empathy. Without a sense of personal identification, the storygoer may grasp the dry gist of an event but sits back, distanced and uninvolved. A turning point's power to merge the meaning of how and why something happened with the emotional impact of the change it caused depends on a sense of shared identity between reader/audience and a principal character.

If the *Iron Man* audience does not identify with Tony Stark, his betrayal by Obadiah Stane may make sense, but no one would care, much less wonder what happens next.

In Action, the center of good, as we noted earlier, is the hero's altruism—her instinct for self-sacrifice. The moment a viewer or reader steps into an Action Story, subconscious instincts whisper: "That hero is like me—a caring human being who willingly risks her life to save victims. Therefore, I want the hero to take action and succeed, because if I were the hero, I would do the same thing." By identifying with altruism and rooting for the hero's fictional success, the storygoer vicariously roots for her own real-life goals. This act of identification releases her pent-up emotions, and she feels the rush of excitement.

EXCITEMENT: THE CORE EMOTION OF ACTION

Core emotion refers to the essential feeling or experience that an audience or reader undergoes while they watch or read a story.

In a Love Story, for instance, longings for love move us to tears. In a Thriller, the core emotion of fear builds in intensity as the protagonist moves closer and closer to death at the hands of a callous criminal. In Horror, terror blazes through an audience as a defenseless victim cringes in the shadow of inexorable evil.

In Action, however, the villain is not a monster and the center of good anchors in a courageous hero rather than a cowering victim. As a result, the high-tension whirl between life and death, between jeopardy and security, actually delights. Like a ride on a plunging roller coaster, we feel a blast of disaster while hugged securely in a harness. Paradoxical as it may seem, this duality of danger and safety, the simultaneity of risk and glee, creates the core emotion of Action: excitement.

Excitement often mixes with other feelings such as hilarity prompted by gags or anger at the collateral damage of a rampaging villain. While other emotions offer enrichments, Action without excitement is like a *T. rex* without teeth.

EMOTIONAL INTENSITY

A red-eyed predator snarling though saliva-dripping jaws excites us . . . in a zoo, behind bars and out of reach. But if the beast escapes, we run screaming for our lives. Excitement, therefore, varies in intensity relative to the immediacy of a threat. As peril gets closer and closer—seconds away, inches away—excitement accelerates. As the menace becomes more and more powerful, more and more vivid, more and more graphic, excitement grows greater and greater.

A well-told Action Story modulates excitement, ramping it up, dialing it down, then ramping it up even higher. The most common pattern opens the story with strong excitement, next quiets to gather power, then follows with cycles of surging/ebbing action that progress dynamically to a final confrontation at climax.

Excitement erupts in five different ways:

FIVE **TECHNIQUES** OF **EXCITEMENT**

1. REBELLION AGAINST **AUTHORITY**
2. CONQUERING **LIMITATIONS**
3. COPING WITH **FRUSTRATION**
4. EXPLORING THE **UNKNOWN**
5. BREAKING **TABOOS**

1. Rebellion Against Authority

Social institutions give authoritative power to those at the top. These people give orders that others must follow. When they abuse this power, rebellion and the rebel who leads it excite us.

2. Exploring the Unknown

Like a wide-eyed child in a dark room, fear in the face of the unseen spurs painful anxieties. Inside a fictional world, the unknown may overwhelm characters with dread, but when watched from the safe distance of fiction, character fright translates into heart-pounding excitement.

3. Coping with Frustration

When a character's immediate goal is within reach, but barriers thwart her, anger is a natural side effect. From a storygoer's point of view, however, the more and more obstacles frustrate a character, pushing her back from a goal that's almost in reach, the more and more excitement charges the scene.

4. Conquering Limitations

In a similar vein, limitations caused by physical and/or temporal forces—a steeper and steeper mountain to climb with less and less time to do it—inspire excitement as each second ticks away and each footstep slips on the rocks.

5. Breaking Taboos

Taboos forbid action. They come haloed with a sense of the sacred, reinforced by the surrounding culture. Breaking a taboo is a kind of blasphemy, as if daring God to strike us dead. That dare sparks excitement.

EXAMPLE: *THE FUGITIVE*

This film's opening sequence packs the first four of these five techniques into a massive charge of excitement.

Richard Kimble, an innocent man convicted of murder and condemned to death row, rides to prison in a bus packed with fellow convicts. Suddenly, the prisoners attempt an escape (technique #1). The bus rolls down a ravine and into the path of an oncoming train. In a race against time, Kimble saves a guard and barely escapes the collision that derails the train (#4).

He flees across the countryside as a US marshal and his deputies give chase (#1). They lose sight of Kimble under a highway overpass. Unseen, he sneaks into a maze of sewage tunnels (#2). The marshals pick up his trail, then lose his trail, then find it again (#3). Finally, Kimble stands at the brink of a towering waterfall, cornered. The marshal orders him to surrender (#1), but he jumps to his seeming death (#4).

CONCLUSION: CONVENTION VERSUS CLICHÉ

As the principal genres evolved, the logic of their design inspired certain settings, roles, events, and values. Over time, audiences and readers came to expect and look forward to these elements as the necessary conventions of that particular type or genre of story: A War Story needs a battlefield (setting); a Love Story needs lovers (roles); a Crime Story needs a crime (event); Action risks Life versus Death (value).

These living features neither shackle the writer nor offer a fail-proof recipe. Conventions simply announce a story's subject matter and then focus curiosity along a spectrum of creative possibilities. However, when an excellent writer's ingenious execution of one of these necessary features achieves a certain perfection, it gets imitated again and again and again. Over time it becomes foreseeable, hollow, and boring—in short, a cliché.

CONVENTION VS. **CLICHE**

GENRE	CONVENTION	CLICHÉ
LOVE STORY	***CORE CAST:*** *Lovers*	X *They meet in a singles bar.*
CRIME STORY	***CORE VALUE:*** *Justice / Injustice*	X *Begins with a dead body found in an alley.*
WAR STORY	***CORE EVENT:*** *A Battle*	X *Protagonist's unit is surrounded.*
ACTION STORY	***CORE ROLE:*** *Villain*	X *The villain is the rich CEO of a corrupt multinational.*

CLASSIC CLICHÉS

In the Love Genre, two lonely people longing for love are the core cast, but when they meet through a dating service, it's a cliché.

In the Crime Genre, Justice/Injustice is the core value, but when injustice begins with a dead body in an alley, it's a cliché.

In the War Genre, the final battle is the core event, but when a fighting unit becomes surrounded, it's a cliché.

In the Action Genre, the villain is a core role, but when she's the massively corrupt multibillionaire CEO of a massively corrupt international corporation, it's a cliché.

Every cliché that infects Action began decades, perhaps centuries ago, as an inspired creative choice that enhanced one of the genre's conventions. This choice, in fact, was so brilliant, lazy writers have recycled it to exhaustion.

To write cliché-free Action, first develop an understanding of the genre's core conventions and a deep respect for the innate purpose of each. Second, research your story's setting, society, history, and principal characters to give yourself a vast knowledge of your subject. Third, use your imagination to explore and expand on everything you know. This hard work gives you creative choices that in turn give you character-specific actions in a setting-specific world. Finally, execute your scenes in ways unique to your vision.

In a one-of-a-kind mercy scene, for instance, your protagonist will outsmart and/or overpower the antagonist in a way no one sees coming, and yet, when it happens, her action will make perfect retroactive sense.

First, research and imagine a one-of-a-kind villain. She is the character to be outsmarted or overpowered. Create a villain so dazzling, so formidable that she cannot be outdone. Second, swing the chessboard around, take the hero's point of view, and beat your own creation. No cheating. Dig deep into your villain and unearth an unseen weakness. Find perhaps a psychological blind spot that in previous scenes looked like a strength but that your hero now perceives as a weakness. Then invent an ingenious way for her to exploit that insight.

PART 2

ACTION CASTS

Role Versus Character

In Chapter Three, we looked at the core cast that makes up the Action Genre—hero, villain, and victim, with their corresponding spirits of altruism, narcissism, and helplessness. But these roles are not characters, at least not yet. A role takes a generic social position within a story (mother, boss, artist, lawyer, loner), then executes a prescribed set of tasks (feeding children, managing staff, painting canvases, defending clients, avoiding people). Like a picture frame around an empty canvas, a role offers the writer a blank space to fill with an original creation.

When hero, villain, and victim enter a story, each assumes a familiar role such as parent, scientist, warrior, cop. As a role executes his tasks, he defines his relationship to the others. When two aspects of his nature contradict each other, he evolves a dimension. Two or more dimensions progress him from flat to complex, from clichéd to creative.

6

THE ACTION TRIAD

CHARACTERIZATION VERSUS TRUE CHARACTER

The term *characterization* describes a role's outer appearances—the physical traits of age, gender, dress, behavior, and voice that strike the storygoer's eye and ear. *True character* names a role's inner nature of morality, mentality, emotionality, and willpower. Because these deep qualities hide unseen in the subtext, the storygoer can only intuit them based on the choices a character makes and the actions he takes.

TRUE CHARACTER IN ACTION ROLES

We are what we do. A character reveals his true self every time he makes a free-will choice in the face of a high-risk, conflict-filled dilemma. What's more, the greater the jeopardy, the truer the choice. When a character stands to lose nothing, his choices and actions may or may not express his true nature. But in the struggle to win it all, when a character stands to lose everything, even his life, his choice of action expresses his essential self. Who is this character at heart? Moral or immoral? Caring or indifferent? Wise or foolish? Cautious or impulsive? Strong or weak? His choices under pressure will tell you.

TRUE CHARACTER IN GAMES

Games are a special case of Action. Gameplay builds story lines and as a result, they pose an interesting question: True character can only be expressed through choices of action in the face of conflict. So, in a game, who makes those revealing choices? Player or protagonist?

Game creators, like screenwriters and novelists, give roles traits of outer characterization. The difference is that in the *as if* worlds of fiction, audiences and readers passively watch empathetic protagonists make free-will choices that expose their deep natures. In games, the protagonist's surface characterization gives him a role to play, but he does so without self-awareness or free will. Therefore, the only minds that make choices and take actions belong to the creator who first invented the game and set its limits, and then the player who plays the game within those limits. A game's protagonist is the embodiment of the player—an avatar without self-awareness, and therefore without an inner self.

For this reason, film adaptations of games often come off as predictable and flat. Their roles had no depth in the game, so they have none on the big screen.

A player, however, as he propels his protagonist, experiences self-revelations, insights that cannot be overstated. In lengthy, highly customizable role-playing games, a player inhabits a character for months if not years, nurturing an intricate, immersive, subconscious involvement unique to the game medium. The greater the number of choices offered the player and the greater the game's capacity to adapt those choices, the greater the depths of complex self-discovery the player experiences.

Can a game creator craft a protagonist who, separate from the player, *seems* to have free will? Who, like a character in a film, play, or novel, makes independent personal choices? Choices that express a hidden, inner nature?

World of Warcraft, a MMORPG (massively multiplayer online role-playing game), offers the player numerous adventures in various locations, while connected to other human players under the watchful eye of a game master. The objective is to reach the maximum level. To do so, a player devises a hero from scratch and characterizes this role with selections of race (nonhuman to human), look (hairstyles to dress styles), class (professions of all kinds), and role (killer to healer).

These choices customize the player's hero, but at the end of the day, no matter how storified role-playing games may seem, the true character they reveal belongs to the player, not his on-screen avatar.

FLAT VERSUS DIMENSIONAL CHARACTERS

The triad hero/villain/victim aligns the hierarchy in an Action Story's society: overdog villain, underdog hero, defenseless victim. Their essential spirits of altruism, narcissism, and helplessness define their core functions, but none of the three can grow from a flat role to a dimensional character until Action merges with at least one presentational genre.

The presentational genre of tone, for example, enriches the Action Genre with a stylistic spectrum that runs from farce to tragedy.

TONAL VARIATIONS IN THE ACTION GENRE

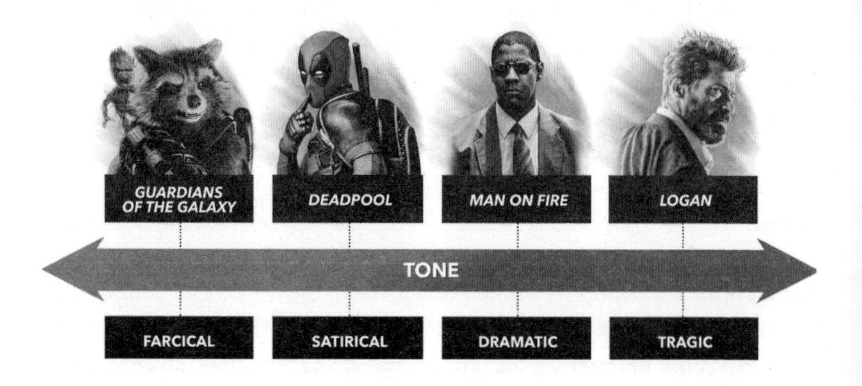

This gives characters a range of tonality that spans from silly to saintly, from farcical (*Guardians of the Galaxy*) to satirical (*Deadpool*) to dramatic (*Man on Fire*) to tragic (*Logan*).

The Ontological Genre offers a spectrum of settings that span from actuality to absurdity.

Most Action Plots take place in a down-to-earth setting, but events could play out in a magical or fantasied or supernatural or nonsensical realm. This range of ontologies offers choices of heroism that stretch from real-life guys like Richard Phillips in *Captain Phillips* to daredevils

ONTOLOGICAL VARIATIONS IN THE ACTION GENRE

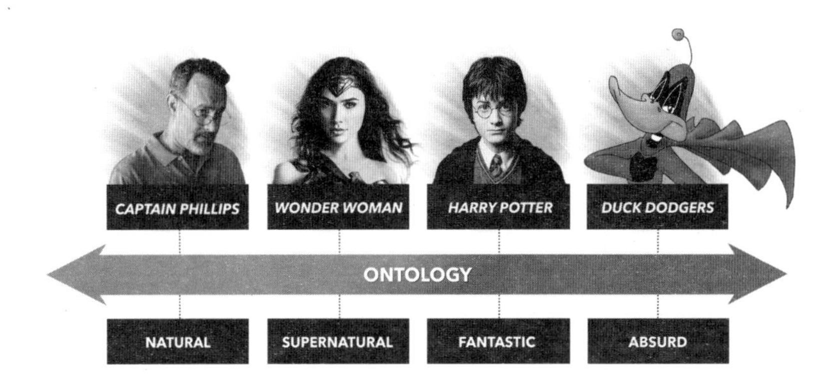

like Bryan Mills in *Taken* to superheroes like Diana Prince in *Wonder Woman* to fantasy heroes like Harry Potter to lunatic heroes like Daffy Duck in *Duck Dodgers in the 24½th Century.*

Action set in a hypothetical future calls for characterizations with some degree of technical know-how. A similar attunement applies to action taking place in the past. Historical characters need to behave in manners true to their period. Animation and Fantasy create timeless worlds that are neither past, present, nor future, but each calls for characters who speak, dress, and behave in a style that fits their imagined world.

Principal genres ground a story's inner components of core value, cast, action, and emotion, while presentational genres express that content outwardly to the audience or reader in an expressive style. When we apply this sense of inner versus outer to a cast of characters, a similar pattern emerges.

DIMENSIONALITY IN ACTION CHARACTERS

A dimension links two contradictory traits within a character. It could span opposite behaviors (a kindly smile versus cruel deeds), disparate physical features (a weak mind in a powerful body), or divergent emotional traits (mirth one day, despair the next) or mental states (a gullible genius). The most common contradictions pit appearances against hidden truths, aspects of characterization against qualities of true character. Someone, for instance, who is physically beautiful but spiritually grotesque.

Over the course of a story, a role's choices and actions expose his true character as he shifts between the positive and negative charges of his dimensions. He might, for example, move from fear-ridden to courageous or the reverse, from cool to impulsive and back to cool, or from loving to cruel until one or the other wins out, thus revealing his essential nature. Character dimensions, therefore, must be consistent and integrated, not momentary and unrelated.

From an audience's or reader's point of view, the push and pull of a character's dimensions fascinate as they wonder which side of a contradiction will come out next, which side will ultimately dominate. As a result, dimensionality makes a character unpredictable and therefore compelling to watch.

THE COMPLEX HERO

The phrase *one-dimensional* does not mean flat. It names a character with a single, hopefully fascinating contradiction in his nature. Many classic Action heroes pivot around one inner/outer dynamic of secret self versus public self.

THE **SECRET IDENTITY** AS **DIMENSION**

Inside the mild-mannered journalist Clark Kent lives his hidden contradiction: Superman. Diana Prince conceals Wonder Woman; Tony

Stark turns into Iron Man; to protect the innocent, Bruce Wayne becomes Batman; Peter Parker does the same as Spider-Man.

Secret identities attract readers and audiences because each of us feels that we, too, harbor a hidden uniqueness—a private self we show no one. This sense of a shared secret draws empathy to a hero. Add to that the hero's altruistic nobility and the audience/reader instinctively identifies with the Action protagonist and roots for his triumph.

A commonly used dimension plays the hero's humanity toward intimates against a brutality toward his nemeses. When Bryan Mills first appeared in the *Taken* trilogy, he embodied this single but powerful dimension: to his family, protective and loving; to his enemies, relentless and lethal.

In *Die Hard*, John McClane fuses two dimensions:

THE **COMPLEX HERO**

JOHN McCLANE

1. Vulnerable to his wife yet hard as nails to his enemies.
2. Devoted to justice yet insubordinate to authority.

In *The Dark Knight*, Batman also flexes two dimensions:

1. Billionaire playboy Bruce Wayne versus the Dark Knight.
2. An inner conflict between a longing to escape his heroic vocation versus his mission to stop the Joker's victimization of Gotham.

Peter Quill acts out three dimensions:

1. When he first appeared in Marvel Comics, he was a galactic policeman, but in *Guardians of the Galaxy* he evolved into the larcenous Star-Lord.
2. His opportunistic wiles keep him coolly distant from other characters, while his inner grief contradicts his nonchalance with a morbid attachment to his dead mother and a hatred of his tyrannical father.
3. His thieving larceny contradicts his humane instincts, but by the end of the day, he puts his instinctive altruism on track and turns hero.

THE **COMPLEX HERO**

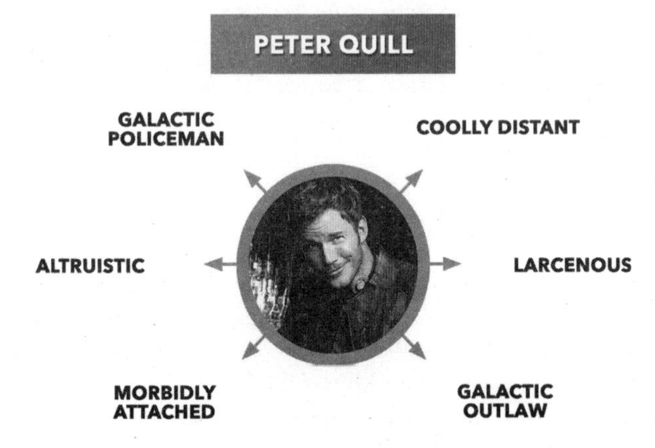

Action roles rarely call for more than two or three dimensions for this reason: Dynamic contradictions often complicate outer struggles with layers of inner turmoil. These unseen conflicts may force an Action hero to turn his back on the life-and-death jeopardies around him while he copes with his inner hell. Every scene he devotes to his demons subtracts from his duel with the story's villain.

Inner conflicts risk killing an Action Story's pace, diminishing the impact of the central conflict and dampening excitement in the audience/reader. And yet, without dimensionality, a predictable mono-behavior flattens into nothing more than a tough-guy pose. For this reason, compelling heroes add another side: Mr. Spock's human side, Ellen Ripley's maternal side, Wall-E's romantic side, Harry Potter's deadly powers, Daenerys Targaryen's fanatical idealism, James Bond's wit.

THE COMPLEX VILLAIN

Heroes don't start fights, villains do. Heroism, therefore, is a reaction to villainy, and an Action Plot's inciting incident does not reach its full impact until the villain's action triggers the hero's reaction. This double event of action/reaction could happen anywhere from the moment the villain first imagines his scheme to his initial step to carry it out to the dark deed itself. At some point along the way, the hero makes a discovery. From the inciting incident on, the villain's plan drives the story's throughline until the hero finally ends it with his climactic action.

The excellence of an Action tale, therefore, ties directly to the quality of the villain and the intense brilliance of his scheme. The more astounding the villain, the more resourceful the hero must become. The more unique the villain's enterprise, the more ingenious the storytelling must become.

THE PSYCHOLOGY OF PATHOLOGY

To create a virtuoso antagonist with a never-seen-before psychopathology, imagine the world from inside a villainous mind. The moment you do, you realize that a villain knows perfectly well that his cause is not moral. Nonetheless, he always believes it is right, justified, and necessary.

The Moral/Immoral spectrum measures a person's attitude toward the needs and desires of other human beings. The altruism at the heart of a hero sets his belief at the positive end of the continuum. Villains, on the other hand, oppose morality. Caring about other people, they believe, is for the weak and foolish.

The Right/Wrong spectrum reflects a person's attitude toward himself—his private needs, his secret desires. The narcissistic mania that grips a villain skews every value back to him. Anything done to fulfill his wants is right; anything that interferes with what he wants is absolutely wrong.

MAGNETISM, REPULSION, MYSTERY

Villainy marshals a triptych of qualities: magnetism, repulsion, mystery. The first two (magnetic/repulsive) brace the villain's dominant dimension.

THE **COMPLEX VILLAIN**

THE **COMPLEX VILLAIN**

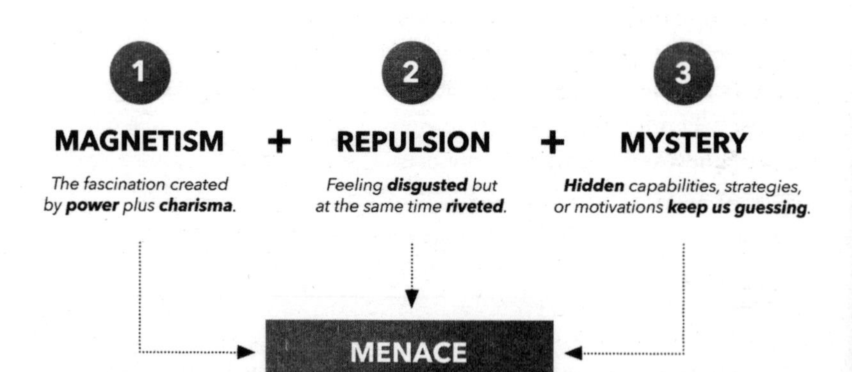

The third (mysterious) marks his key trait. Taken together, the three radiate an intriguing sense of menace.

As spectators to Action, we are attracted to power yet abhorrent of evil. Both qualities radiate from a well-written villain and, therefore, fascinate us. Add a cloak of secrets, and a villain will first captivate us, and then surprise us with revelation after revelation until he becomes the character we love to hate.

Let's examine these three qualities.

1. Magnetic

Power plus charisma fascinates the audience/reader. For many of us, the great villains—Hannibal Lecter, Darth Vader, Anton Chigurh, the Joker, T-1000, HAL 9000, Henry Drax—stand near the top of our favorite characters.

Die Hard's charismatic Hans Gruber has no delusions that what he's doing is for anyone's benefit but his own. No matter how homicidal his criminal scheme, he takes pride in his ingenious theft, kills without conscience, and through it all savors his brilliance . . . as do we.

2. Repulsive

We feel disgust when staring into a twisted mind and its gross desires; yet at the same time, we're riveted and dare not look away.

In *Mission: Impossible—Ghost Protocol*, Kurt Hendricks, aka Cobalt, breeds this villainous dimension of fascination/disgust by inverting values. He believes he's not only right but moral. He wants to create a nuclear holocaust that will eliminate civilization so that the human race can start over and this time get it right. In other words, for the good of humanity he would incinerate humanity. He wraps riveting evil inside warped insanity.

3. Mysterious

A villain needs secrets. The wise Action writer keeps his villain's powers hidden, revealing them one at a time in order of increasing wonder and effect, each at the worst possible moment for the hero and the best possible surprise for the audience/reader. For without covert strengths, a villain cannot turn scenes with the sudden, well-timed revelations that catch the eye and shock the mind. As a result, his actions become predictable and dull.

Terminator 2: Judgment Day: The T-1000 first appears as a cop dealing with a disturbance—until a shotgun blast rips him open, exposing his glistening, silvery innards. From then on, this liquid metal robot amazes us with his ingenious shapeshifting secrets. At first, we think he can only transform into human figures, but scene by scene, reveal by reveal, we discover he can become anything—even a floor made of black-and-white tiles.

In *The Dark Knight*, the Joker appears in Gotham from seemingly out of nowhere, hiding his identity behind a grotesque makeup. When someone stares at his hideously scarred face, he says, "You wanna know how I got these scars? My father was a drunk and a gambler." Later, however, he blames his disfigurements on an ex-wife.

With his first lie, the Joker manipulates us with a claim of child abuse; with his second, he adds fuel with hostility to women. His psychological gamesmanship amplifies both his menace and magnetism, while adding to his mystery: How, in fact, did he get those scars?

Some villains, of course, are simply amoral. The shark in *Jaws* is neither right nor wrong nor good nor bad... just hungry. Film audiences, however, invest it with the spirit of evil and interpret its immense power as diabolical, even sadistic. The shark's only mystery is one of scale. We wonder if its rage knows any limit.

A villain without a hint of mystery and lacking the core dimension of attraction versus loathing bores us. Consider Joffrey Baratheon. The *Game of Thrones* screenwriters did not want a true villain in this role but rather an annoying, weak, flawed scoundrel. So, they simply reversed the three key traits of villainy. Instead of magnetic, they made Joffrey irritating; instead of mysterious, they made him shallow; most important, instead of repulsive, they made him whiny until he finally and gratefully choked to death on poison.

THE COURAGEOUS VILLAIN

Villains can have many positive traits: tenacity, confidence, self-awareness. What's more, they are not bullies. Bullies are cowards who abuse the weak. Villains take on heroes. They often preen and brag about their schemes, certain that no intelligence can match their own; no power, no moral authority surpasses them. What's more, their courage is real. As Ahab says in *Moby-Dick*, "I would strike the sun if it insulted me."

And yet, even though a villain has the guts of a marine, he does not draw empathy. For good reason. An empathic villain turns Action on its head. When we stare into the heart of a villain, we're not looking for a soul mate. We're simply fascinated with the workings of evil. We may stand in awe of Hannibal Lecter but never think the thought: "He's just like me."

THE VILLAIN'S PLAN

A villain is only as villainous as his stratagem. The three qualities of magnetism, repulsiveness, and mystery characterize not only him but his scheme as well.

Nothing is more important to a villain than his plan. He has devoted an immense amount of creative energy to its complex conception, time-consuming preparations and (from the reader/audience's point of view) mysterious yet fascinating deceptions. To him, it's an ingenious work of criminal art. Others will find his plan hideous and inhuman, but his emotions swell with the liberating euphoria that comes from abandoning morality. Freed of conscience, he becomes a slave to this grand design. He cannot turn away from it; he cannot rise above it. He will risk or even sacrifice his life to achieve it.

THE DIMENSIONLESS VICTIM

An Action cast needs to maintain a sure balance between hero and villain: Heroes possess more emotional interest and empathy, while villains possess more menace and power. The Action writer can tilt this balance any way he wishes, but an extreme imbalance caused by an utterly unstoppable hero or a kindly compassionate villain risks disappointment and confusion.

To maintain balance in an Action Story, victims rarely develop a dimension and certainly not one that might open the door to escape. If a victim possessed dimensions such as resourceful/resourceless, clever/inept, skilled/unskilled, or powerful/powerless, he could draw on his positive capabilities and eventually find the wherewithal to bolt or retaliate. If he does, the story's villain becomes incompetent and its hero pointless.

PLURAL ROLES

Heroes, villains, and victims can be cast as duos, trios, or groups of almost any size.

The dimensions of a lone Action hero seem limited to two or three, but this role becomes immediately more complex when cast as an ensemble. Heroes often come in pairs: Batman and Robin, Butch Cassidy and the Sundance Kid, Agents K and J, and even bickering duets such as Cosmo and Rocket Raccoon. Teams of heroes range from a handful in *The Magnificent Seven* to over sixty in *Justice League Unlimited* to the 300.

Many villains also team up, as do René Belloq and Arnold Toht in *Raiders of the Lost Ark*, the Penguin and the Riddler in *Gotham*, and the trio of General Zod, Faora, and Jax-Ur in *Man of Steel*. Some villains add cohorts numbering from gangs on street corners to the massive swarms of aliens in *A Quiet Place* and *Independence Day*.

The same goes for victims. They can multiply from a family held for ransom to entire planetary populations: *Star Trek*, *Ghost Protocol*, *The Matrix*.

CHANGING ROLES

Roles are not necessarily fixed throughout a telling. Magneto, for instance, switches from conflicted hero to chief villain in *X-Men: Days of Future Past*. *Looper* plots a double switch as a time paradox splits the protagonist into two versions of the same self. Young Joe begins the story as a self-centered villain who cares nothing for anyone, not even his future self. Old Joe, however, travels back in time to risk his life to kill someone who will one day become a mass-murdering crime boss. Gradually, these two characters switch roles. At climax, an altruistic Young Joe sacrifices himself to save the victims of the now villainous Old Joe.

So long as role changes seem fully motivated and credible, we will follow characters in any direction, even circles. In *The Last Jedi*, Kylo Ren switches from conflicted villain to hero, but then, disappointed with that role, pivots back to ruthless villain.

HYBRID ROLES

Just as a group of characters can play one role, a single character can combine two roles into one. Action offers four possible combinations:

HYBRID ROLES IN ACTION

Possess both an ***altruistic spirit*** *and a kind of* ***helplessness****.*

1. Hero-Victim

This character possesses spirits of both helplessness and altruism. And when they merge, the role alternates between the fear of captivity and the courage of self-sacrifice.

In *The Fugitive*, when the security van taking Richard Kimble to prison crashes, he risks his chance for freedom to save a bleeding prison guard. Backed to the edge of a storming precipice, he defies a US marshal and jumps a thousand feet into a gorge of roaring water. While hiding in a hospital, searching for clues to his wife's murderer, he risks capture to save a dying patient who was left unattended.

In the backstory of the Action/Fantasy game *The Legend of Zelda: Breath of the Wild*, the hero-victim Princess Zelda imprisons herself along with the villain Ganon in order to save Link and the land of Hyrule.

In *No Country for Old Men*, Llewelyn Moss stumbles on the blood-soaked aftermath of a drug deal gone bad. As he grabs a stash of cash, he notices a wounded gangster moaning, still alive. Unable to sleep that night, his conscience drives him back to the crime scene to save the dying man. Suddenly, the cartel shows up, searching for their money.

Moss goes on the run until the story's villain, Anton Chigurh, tracks him down. Chigurh makes Moss an offer: If Moss gives up the money, he won't execute Moss's wife. Moss rejects the deal and vows to kill Chigurh. Moss, unfortunately, is fatally out of his league. Cartel thugs soon gun him down as Chigurh assassinates his wife. Moss is as altruistic as any hero but as helpless as a victim.

HYBRID ROLES IN ACTION

*Counterpoints **altruism** with **narcissism**. Willing to **sacrifice his life** to save victims and yet **sacrifices victims** to his cause.*

2. Hero-Villain

The hero-villain fusion counterpoints altruism with narcissism to create a character who's willing to sacrifice his life to save victims and yet sacrifices victims to his cause. In a series such as *Vikings*, warriors risk their lives for their culture and mercilessly butcher anyone outside it. In many stories, this conflicted nature wages a moral war within a character until he sacrifices himself for the very people he exploited.

The hero-villain merger often calls for a fanatic. In the Marvel Universe, Magneto evolves from supervillain to antihero to superhero. Soon after World War II, he launches his furious crusade for mutant liberation, heroically risking his life for his fellow nonhumans. Anyone opposing his cause, even other mutants such as the X-Men, becomes his victim. Then, in *X-Men: Days of Future Past*, Magneto joins the X-Men, risking his life to fight on their side in a last-ditch battle against the Sentinels.

Daniel Dravot in *The Man Who Would Be King* embodies this core contradiction. Thanks to a stroke of coincidence, the people of an Afghan province believe that Dravot is the reincarnation of Alexander the Great. Leveraging their trust along with his skills as a British soldier, he installs himself as king, then plots to plunder his victims and return to England a wealthy man. Instead, he trades the greed of colonialism for the ideals of civilization and decides to rule with justice. He tries to help his victims, but they see through his deceit and end his life.

3. Victim-Villain

The villain-victim merger calls for a complex dimension that contradicts the narcissism of the villain with the helplessness of the victim. This

HYBRID ROLES IN ACTION

*Contrasts the **narcissism** of the villain with the **helplessness** of the victim. Often **caught up in events** they set in motion.*

paradoxical hybrid creates a character who endangers the lives of others and yet ends up as helpless as his victims.

In *Captain Phillips*, Muse, an impoverished Somalian turned pirate, commandeers an American freighter. Despite his clever planning and courage, Muse has no defense against the overwhelming might of the US Navy. Trapped by his own decisions, his shipmates are killed and he's captured. The events Muse set into motion sweep both the pirate villain and freighter captain into the helpless victim role.

In *The Lord of the Rings*, Gollum becomes the pitiable victim of the evil Sauron, yet he treacherously and ruthlessly victimizes Frodo and Sam.

4. Hero-Villain-Victim

A hero-villain-victim combines altruism and narcissism with helplessness.

The Incredible Hulk: When Bruce Banner transforms into the Hulk, he becomes a villainous nightmare killing innocents in his path, and yet a

HYBRID ROLES IN ACTION

A character playing all three roles combines ***altruism*** *and* ***narcissism*** *with* ***helplessness****.*

hero desperate to protect people from himself and a victim of his doppelgänger. In the last act, however, he deliberately summons the Hulk and risks his life to save humanity from the Abomination. By story's end, Banner controls the Hulk and so joins a team of heroes.

In the many versions of *King Kong*, a giant ape destroys those who dare challenge him, yet risks his life for the person he loves, and ends up chained, humiliated, riddled with bullets, plunging to his death.

A character could evolve from a bystander or from a supporting role into a core character, then shift from one role to another and back again.

The Empire Strikes Back: Lando Calrissian first appears as the suave, wealthy owner of Cloud City and supporter of the heroes' cause. But he betrays them and sells out to Darth Vader. Vader's tyranny over Cloud City soon reduces this turncoat to a victim. Lando then rebels, freeing the heroes and joining their ensemble.

In an origin story, such as Spider-Man's, an everyday character transitions into a hero. *The Incredibles* pivots the opposite movement as a former hero turned working dad reclaims his mantle. Magneto, as we noted, changes from hero to villain and back again. The fun in *Face/Off* comes when Castor Troy and Sean Archer switch identities and, with that, their roles as hero and villain.

These hybrids raise a structural problem: What becomes of the mercy scene? How can a villain-victim put a hero at his mercy? For that matter, how can a hero-villain put himself at his mercy?

In one solution, numerous characters play the villain. *The Lord of the Rings*, for instance, brims with villains until the One Ring itself ultimately motivates the mercy scene and takes Gollum to his death.

In a telling with multiple heroes, a character might transform from a hero to a villain who then turns on one of the other heroes. Magneto, for example, goes full-villain at the climax of both *X-Men: First Class* and *X-Men: Days of Future Past* to create the mercy scene for each.

MERGED ROLES

The only roles essential to Action storytelling are hero, villain, and victim. Professions such as detective and criminal, spy and terrorist, scientist and alien are characterizations borrowed from other genres and merged with an Action cast to motivate events.

Series such as *Lethal Weapon* and *Men in Black* add an Action central plot to the tonal genre of Comedy as well as subplots of Crime and Buddy Salvation. These mixtures and mergers characterize altruistic heroes as bantering detectives, adding traits of wit and comradery to the analytical skills of a sleuth.

POLARIZED ROLES

Outside of Action's three core roles, the rest of the cast either helps or hinders. Those who help the hero—sidekicks, co-workers, experts—hinder the villain. Those who help the villain—henchmen, bumbling bureaucrats, headline-hungry reporters—hinder the hero. Anyone can get in the way and hinder the hero or drop a clue on the path to help him. In a well-designed Action cast, no one is neutral.

Consider the core cast of *Die Hard*: John McClane takes on the hero role; Hans Gruber plays the villain; Holly McClane, her boss, Mr. Takagi, and two dozen corporate employees are all victims.

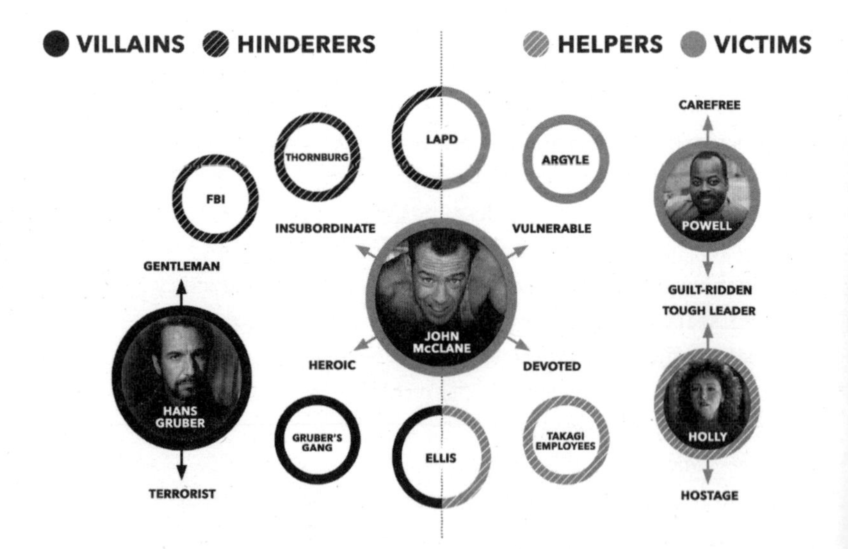

The expanded cast features those who help McClane: McClane's driver, Argyle, and Powell, the first cop on the scene. Argyle helps block the villains' escape and Powell kills the last of Gruber's gang. But then, from every possible angle, come those who hinder McClane: the reporter Richard Thornburg who reveals Holly's identity, giving Gruber leverage over McClane; the FBI who unwittingly help Gruber break into the Nakatomi vault; the LAPD's bureaucracy that puts cops in jeopardy, forcing McClane to risk his life to save them. Ellis, a victim, unwittingly endangers McClane by trying to broker a deal with Gruber.

These supporting roles help delineate McClane's character. When he confides his worries and fears to Argyle and Powell, we sense his vulnerability. Yet, when he confronts Gruber, he exudes confidence and unflinching bravery. McClane is unshakably devoted to the terrified victims but insubordinate to the bumbling LAPD and FBI.

In the very complex cast of *Guardians of the Galaxy*, almost every helper—Yondu, the Nova Corps, the Broker, the Collector—doubles as a hinderer. In fact, the heroic guardians unwittingly hinder themselves.

MISSING ROLES

The core cast of Action forms a triangle with a purpose. It gives its hero a victim to save and a villain to defeat. Without a victim, a hero cannot be heroic nor a villain villainous. Although these principles seem obvious, many Action works suffer from an absent victim or villain or both.

A victim under the threat of death should summon a sense of compassion from the audience/reader, but when there's no victim to live or die, an Action Story becomes pointless and emotionless.

In *Thor: Ragnarok*, the only candidates for victimhood are the godlike inhabitants of Asgard. In *X-Men Origins: Wolverine*, the death of Kayla Silverfox seals the Love Story subplot, but she is not a vulnerable victim. She wields a superpower, the tactohypnotic ability to mesmerize anyone she touches. Silverfox dies a hero. Without a true victim, Action has little chance of engaging excitement.

Unbreakable never fills the villain role. The two children who might have served as the victims end up saving the hero's life instead.

In the film *2012*, a solar flare heats the Earth's core, which in turn causes an inflammation of the Earth's crust, which in turn causes a cataclysmic wipeout of all of humankind, thus making the victim role duller than livestock. Without compassion, repetitious images of destruction, no matter how spectacular, punish the audience with gratuitous disaster, the very opposite of excitement.

7

POWER

To maintain life, all living things conserve energy. Why would any creature do anything the hard, dangerous way if it can get what it wants in an easy, secure way? It won't. Nothing ever does. No living thing ever spends a single calorie it doesn't have to, changes in any way it doesn't need to, takes any risks it can avoid, does more than it must, if it can get what it wants in a simple, secure, painless, effort-least way. The first law of nature is the conservation and preservation of life.

The human mind is nature's only self-aware being, but nonetheless, like all living things, it obeys the first law. What will cause a protagonist's conservative instincts to rise to the occasion and become the fully realized, intriguing, empathic character you hope to create? The answer lies on the negative side of the story.

THE PRINCIPLE OF ANTAGONISM

Conflict is to story what sound is to music, what movement is to dance, what shape is to architecture. Without antagonistic forces in moment-by-moment conflict, a story hangs like a still life on a wall—worth a look, even a good look, but then you move on.

Hero and villain define each other. Like mirrors on opposite walls, an aspect of one reflects the reverse in the other. The villain's narcissism contradicts the hero's altruism; the villain's cruelty offsets the hero's empathy. At the apex of antagonism, the villain's overwhelming power crushes the hero's last reserves.

The extent to which a character becomes intellectually fascinating and emotionally compelling depends on the negative forces that block her from getting what she wants. As these sources of antagonism increase in power and complexity, she is compelled to reach for deeper and deeper resources that lift her above and beyond herself.

The more powerful the forces of antagonism, the more the protagonist must reach into her creative imagination, the more she must muster sides of herself she's never known before, the more brilliant she must become—all in a final struggle to destroy the villain.

THE NEGATION OF THE NEGATION

The core value at the heart of each principal genre strikes a binary charge of positive versus negative energy. By *positive*, we mean life-affirming and creative; by *negative*, we mean death-fixated and destructive. The core value in the War Story is Victory/Defeat; in the Crime Story, Justice/Injustice; in the Love Story, Love/Hate; in Action, Life/Death; and so on through the other basic story forms. In each principal genre, an empathetic protagonist represents and acts out the value's positive charge, while the story's antagonistic characters portray the negative side.

A story's sources of conflict flow along a spectrum of negative energies that runs from slight to absolute with every possible shade of villainy in between. In situations such as a stalemate in a War Story, indifference in a Love Story, or bureaucratic unfairness in a Crime Story, the protagonist faces a force of antagonism that's contrary to the positive charge. By *contrary*, we mean a negative force that's somewhat but not fully opposite, not yet contradictory.

When negative forces escalate to defeat or hate or injustice respectively, they inflict an impact that's directly opposed to the positive. In this contradictory state, however, no matter how much blood such conflicts spill, the absolute limit of human suffering has not been reached.

Human beings are very resourceful, very inventive. They know how to multiply destructive power beyond the opposite charge of value and build a negative state that isn't just quantitatively worse, not just more and more of the same, but qualitatively worse, a darker intensity of a wholly new kind on a wholly new scale.

In a Crime Story, a criminal's act of injustice contradicts justice, but the law still rules. A cop could solve the crime, apprehend the criminal, and return society to a lawful state. But suppose tyranny corrupts a society's institutions and crime becomes the norm. In these authoritarian worlds, the law turns toothless and only might makes right.

In a War Story, defeat quashes victory, but suppose, as in George Orwell's *1984*, that a government perverts the minds of its citizens by rebranding a grisly downfall as a glorious triumph. When a country wins battles but forfeits its humanity, as did Germany in World War II, moral defeat is far worse than surrender; it warps a nation's soul.

In a Love Story, hate-filled acts contradict love and destroy a relationship. But suppose the failed romantic then turns her loathing against the only person left to care about, herself. If self-love twists into self-hate, she drives her life over an emotional cliff.

In an Action Story, death contradicts life. Death is negative but natural. We are all going to die. So, what's worse than death? First, an unnatural, premature death by murder, especially on a massive scale. Second, death masquerading as life, such as Cobalt's plan in *Ghost Protocol* to give mankind rebirth by destroying all civilization. Third, damnation: a state of hideous suffering extended through eternity that turns death, going out of existence, into an act of mercy.

THE BALANCING ACT

In Action, the power of villainy cannot equal the power of heroism. The two must be radically imbalanced in favor of villainy. In the last four examples, the villain's negation of the hero's positive energy was negated a second time with great effect as the dark forces of evil built to an overwhelming negation of the negation. This doubly negative power forced the hero, in a final effort to win, to reach as deep and wide as humanly possible into the far limits of brains and brawn. (For more on the negation of the negation, see *Story: Substance, Structure, Style, and the Principles of Screenwriting*, pages 317–333.)

HERO AS UNDERDOG

Action casts its hero as an underdog for many reasons. First, empathy.

All human beings, even those atop massive institutions, see themselves as underdogs. This back-to-the-wall feeling is an instinctive reaction to the travails that block our path through life.

When an audience member senses that the conflicts of a fictional underdog mirror her labors in the real world, she empathizes with the hero's humanity. This sense of mutual identity draws her into the telling as if it were happening to her, exciting her from scene to scene. For that reason, an overdog hero winning fight after fight against a dim-witted thug is as boring as a juggler spinning plates.

The second and equally important reason: suspense. An Action Story must constantly pose questions about its future turning points: What's going to happen next? And after that? How will this turn out? At the same time, however, Action storygoers know by tradition what will ultimately happen. With very few exceptions, the outcome will be positive, and the villain will suffer defeat at the hands of the hero. That awareness tends to diminish their curiosity.

Action suspense, therefore, also questions the *hows* and *whys* of things. When witnessing a mercy scene, for example, the audience/reader knows that the hero will turn tables on the villain. But it does not know how she will do it. What hidden resource will she call on? Her wits? Her muscle? A hidden talent?

Action writing is a kind of literary Cirque du Soleil: A hero must be an underdog with minimal, at times futile resources, and yet never seem as weak as a victim—a tightrope walk of character design. And yet no matter a hero's skills, which in certain characters can be awesome, the villain must possess even greater prowess—another high-wire feat.

Consider the balancing act in *Mission: Impossible—Ghost Protocol*.

The writers turn their tough-as-nails heroes into in-over-their-heads underdogs by creating character dimensions unlike any previous *MI* film. Each of the four IMF team members develops an inner contradiction between power and weakness.

First, Benji, an expert in high-tech, bumbles and babbles like a nervous amateur when pressure builds. Second, Carter's guilt over the death of Hanaway, her mission partner and lover, riddles her with doubt. Third, Brandt pretends to be a data analyst when he is not. Fourth, in the opening sequence, Ethan Hunt, the IMF's top agent, becomes wildly impulsive as the team rescues him from a Russian prison. Once on the mission, his physical skills seem suspect as he injures himself repeatedly.

THE **HERO** AS **UNDERDOG**

The unraveling of the backstory of how he ended up in a Russian prison makes the other three wonder if Ethan has become unhinged.

The negative sides of these four characters—bumbling inexperience, self-doubt, phony identity, recklessness—weaken and reduce the team to underdogs. Plus, things go wrong. The gadgets that made the IMF famous, such as their rubber mask disguises and self-destructing communication devices, fail when needed most. All this leads to faulty teamwork and bickering.

The screenwriters then pit this struggling team against Cobalt, a psychotic villain who blows up the Kremlin and a thousand lives with it, and then cleverly pins the bombing on the United States. He ingeniously evades pursuit across the globe and finally fires a nuclear weapon at San Francisco.

VILLAIN AS OVERDOG

Weak forces of antagonism do not generate excitement in any story, let alone Action. Therefore, when weighed against the hero, the villain must wield enormous power. If a villain flush with power towers over a hero stripped of power, empathetic audiences and readers feel a rush of emotion-charged curiosity. As the odds against the hero soar with each desperate risk of life, adrenaline flows. Extreme overdog/underdog imbalance sets the platform for action-filled scenes and triggers excitement.

To take the underdog versus overdog principle to its limit, consider superheroes. Why would a character gifted with supreme powers ever kneel at mercy of a villain? How does Superman, for instance, become an underdog to his three prime enemies: Lex Luthor, General Zod, and Brainiac?

Superman: The Movie: Lex Luthor paralyzes Superman with kryptonite, then locks him in a spatial dilemma: Luthor launches two nuclear rockets in opposite directions—one aimed at Hackensack, New Jersey, the other at the San Andreas Fault with an aim to cause an earthquake that will push California into the ocean. Superman saves Hackensack, and then flies into the splintering San Andreas Fault, fusing California back to the North American continent through the friction of his own body. No small task.

The earthquake, however, has killed Lois Lane. Now Superman faces a moral dilemma: He can either obey his father's sacred commandment against interference in human destiny or save the woman he loves. He chooses the latter. Superman leverages quantum mechanics, reverses the spin of the planet, turns back time, and resurrects Lois.

Superman: The Man of Steel: In Superman's origin story, General Dru-Zod, a megalomaniacal Kryptonian military chief, plans to abolish Earth by using a massive World Engine to terraform the planet into a neo-Krypton. Superman destroys the World Engine, and then defeats Zod in a hand-to-hand battle. *Superman II* picks up from the origin story and brings Zod back, this time with two Kryptonian cohorts, reducing the Man of Steel to an underdog by outnumbering him three supervillains to one superhero.

Superman: The Animated Series: Brainiac, a super-conscious computer, downloads the total knowledge of Kryptonian civilization into the memory banks of a spaceship, then embodies itself in an android and escapes moments before the planet explodes. In a later episode, when Superman discovers Brainiac's plan to destroy Earth, he crushes the vessel that houses the memory banks, thinking that killing its computers will kill it. But an episode later, Superman discovers that Brainiac downloaded itself into Lex Luthor's computers, then forced Luthor to give it a new android body.

Of the three villains, Lex Luthor inflicts the greatest negative force because he has mastered the power of dilemma. Zod and Brainiac make

Superman risk his life, but Luthor makes him choose between two evils: the violation of his father's code or the death of the woman he loves. In this impasse, no matter what action Superman takes, it will cost him something he loves.

The most powerful villains turn a hero into an underdog by manipulating her into a no-win situation that makes her pay a price for any choice.

THE **HERO'S VULNERABILITY** TO THE VILLAIN

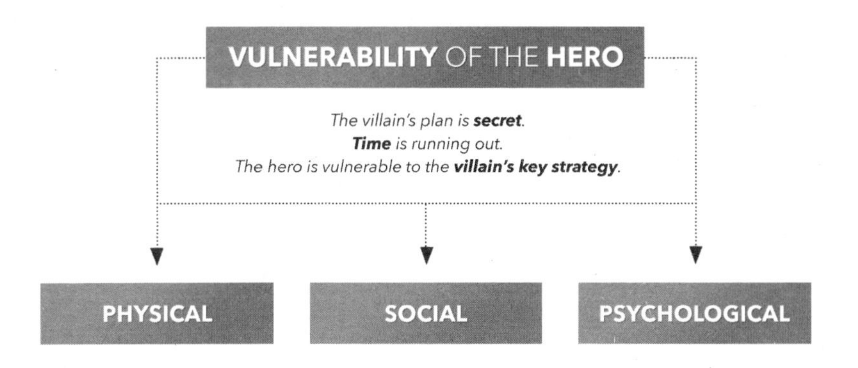

Flaws often make a hero more human, more multifaceted, although in Action, one or two dimensions is complexity enough. A hero does not need a specific weakness to make her vulnerable. What's crucial is the villain's weapon. It must work, especially on the hero. For no matter her skills or power, a hero must be vulnerable to the villain's key tactic.

This vulnerability could be physical, sociological, or psychological.

Physical

Action's most famous physical susceptibility is Superman's to kryptonite, making a seemingly invulnerable hero vulnerable.

THE **HERO'S VULNERABILITY**

Social

In *John Wick* films, hired killers treat every Continental hotel in the world as a realm of enforced neutrality. Inside the hotel's premises, all assassins must cease all violence. The hotel owners, such as Winston in New York City, enforce this law, and for reasons never revealed, all members of the international assassin profession, John Wick included, feel honor-bound to keep it (until they transgress).

THE **HERO'S VULNERABILITY**

Psychological

THE **HERO'S VULNERABILITY**

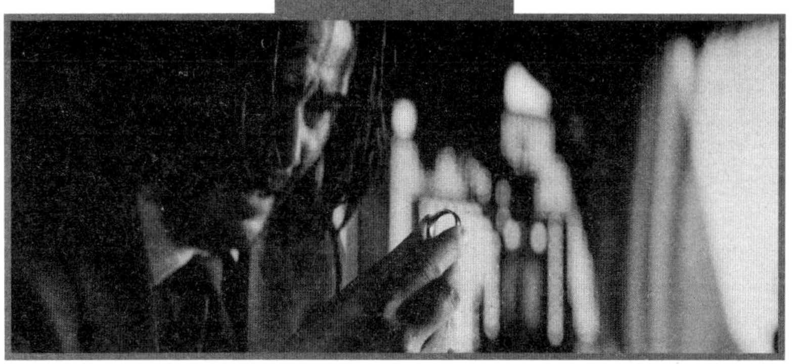

A hero's weakness could be phobic, such as Indiana Jones's fear of snakes. In *The Dark Knight*, Batman's secret identity protects him from organized crime, but the Joker's psychological insight burrows through his guise. When he orders Batman to turn himself in or he'll start blowing up hospitals, Batman's conscience pulls the mask off Bruce Wayne.

In a more mysterious vein, in *John Wick: Chapter 3—Parabellum*, the High Table, a committee of twelve international crime bosses, sets a $14 million bounty on Wick. Wick seeks out the Elder, the mysterious Moroccan head of the High Table. For reasons never explained, Wick is psychologically defenselessness against this supremely powerful mind. The Elder tells Wick to cut off his ring finger and hand over his wedding band—a symbol of Wick's one true love, his late wife, Helen. Wick submits and the Elder annuls the bounty.

VILLAIN'S INVULNERABILITY TO THE HERO

No matter what skills a hero brings to the conflict, an Action villain is immune to them. As a result, the villain cannot be assassinated or even intimidated. Faced with an impervious villain, a hero must exhaust one

THE **VILLAIN'S INVULNERABILITY** TO THE HERO

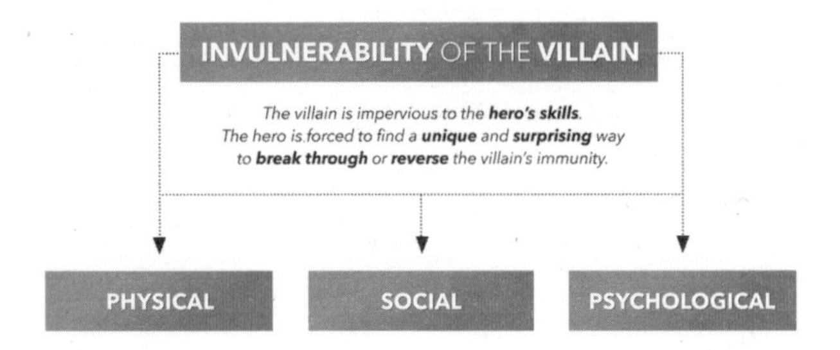

gambit after another, with no guarantee of success. As her tactics turn more and more desperate, her strategic ideas fade, her chances vanish.

From this dwindling position, the hero must defiantly persist, dig deeper, and discover not just new techniques but new talents within herself as well. Suspense explodes into excitement as we watch a tenacious hero devise a unique, surprising way to break through a villain's immunity or invent a quick-minded improvisation that turns a villain's invulnerability inside out.

Villainous immunity could be physical, sociological, or psychological.

Physical

Consider *Terminator 2: Judgment Day*. The primary tactic of the hero, the T-800, is massive physical strength backed by high-powered long

THE **VILLAIN'S INVULNERABILITY**

guns. But the shapeshifting, liquid metal body of the T-1000 swallows punches without a ripple, while shotgun blasts barely slow it down. This villain seems indestructible.

Spider-Man's villains, such as the Lizard, Doctor Octopus, Venom, and Green Goblin, simply tear his webs apart. Sandman grins as the webs go right through him.

Social

THE **VILLAIN'S INVULNERABILITY**

The second source of immunity draws on social dynamics. In *Die Hard*, John McClane is a cop from New York City. When he flashes his badge on those streets and says, "You're under arrest," suspects hold out their arms and he snaps on cuffs. So, when he first confronts one of the villain's team, he tries to make an arrest. Hans Gruber laughs at the idea. His gang obeys no law. They need killing, not jailing. This forces McClane to change tactics and become a guerrilla fighter in a high-rise.

Psychological

Batman's chief weapon is his intimidating, dark persona. Yet his enemies never flinch, least of all the Joker. When the Dark Knight interrogates the Joker in a police station, he laughs in Batman's face. The more Batman hits him, the more the Joker enjoys it.

THE **VILLAIN'S INVULNERABILITY**

INSTITUTIONAL POWERS

The balance of power within human relationships is almost never equal. One side nearly always possesses higher status or strength or resources than the other. These unequal relationships need not be corrupt or undeserved or oppressive; parents have power over their children, bosses over employees, teachers over students.

To elevate a villain to an overdog, Action writers often give this role institutional power in one of five variations:

1. Imbalance Inside the Same Institution

If hero and villain work within the same social structure, then the higher the level, the greater the power. The villain need not be at the highest rank, just substantially above the hero.

In *The Bourne Identity*, Jason Bourne works under a villainous CIA director.

2. Unequal Levels Within Different Institutions

If the villain and hero operate within separate structures, the villain gains power by reigning higher in his institution than the hero does in his.

In *Die Hard*, John McClane, a New York detective, duels with Hans Gruber, head of an international crime consortium.

3. A Lesser Institution Inside a Greater Institution

The hero may head his own minor institution within a major institution that gives the villain superlative power.

In *Star Wars*, Luke and the Rebel Alliance wage a galactic civil war against the vast power of the Empire. In *The Incredibles*, Mr. Incredible, his family's husband and father, works for the story's villain, a gigantic corporation run by Syndrome.

4. A Small Team Against a Huge Institution

This strategy often becomes a drama of numbers. In stories such as *The Seven Samurai*, *The Magnificent Seven*, *300*, and *The Three Musketeers*, teams of heroes battle armies of villains. In the Action/Sci-Fi game series *Halo*, Master Chief John-117's lone partner is his AI companion Cortana.

To make the power disparity all the greater, Action tellings frequently pit one against many, casting the hero as a loner, a team of one: *Shane*, *The Outlaw Josey Wales*, *Mad Max 2: The Road Warrior*. In *Shadow*, Jingzhou, an untrained commoner, duels Yang Cang, the warrior king of a mighty, fortified city.

Stories that begin with the villain as head of an institution come with a risk: Because the villain possesses overwhelming strength, her singular tactics may become repetitious and predictable, forcing the writer to find ingenious ways to turn scenes with surprise.

To demonstrate a villain's institutional power, the writer often gives her masses of henchmen, but as more and more bodies pile up, repetition breeds boredom. To build excitement, consider giving an institution-powered villain a special weapon as well, a one-of-a-kind power, such as a secret technology that sees things no one else can.

5. A Lone Villain Versus a Hero's Institution

In *Mission: Impossible—Ghost Protocol*, Cobalt manipulates the rival governments of the US and Russia on a vast scale and subverts their powers. He maneuvers the United States into abandoning the IMF, strips the team of their technical gear, blows up the Kremlin, sends Russian operatives on a manhunt for Ethan, commandeers an atomic submarine, and launches a nuclear missile.

Some villains seize power over the course of the story. In *The Dark Knight*, the Joker starts out as a petty thief, but piece by piece, murder by murder, this psychopath takes over the city's mafia and holds Gotham for ransom. This less-to-more progression dramatizes the villain's rise to power and greatly increases excitement.

INSTITUTIONAL VILLAINY

A social institution focuses its purpose through a specific value. To protect citizens, governments face Threat versus Security conflicts. Creative talents grapple with the Beauty/Banality struggle at the heart of every art form. In institutions of higher learning, scholars battle Ignorance with Knowledge. Religions pit Morality against Immorality. And at the pinnacle of each stands a leader committed to the institution's core value... or so we would like to think.

Villains corrupt an organization by inverting its core value from an

HOW VILLAINS **CORRUPT INSTITUTIONS**

absolute positive charge to an absolute negative. Let's, for example, trace the corruption of an institution founded on Justice/Injustice through four progressive stages:

1. Unfairness

As a first step, a villain might increase her power by deceiving the board of directors into firing a rival. The villain's unethical tactic degrades the institution's values from justice to unfairness, but at that point, she has not broken the law.

2. Injustice

In the next step, however, she does. Using her new position, she steals high-tech secrets from the R&D department, sells them to another corporation, then cleverly pins the theft on an innocent victim. The villain's scheme goes undetected as the unwitting institution moves from unfairness to injustice.

3. Tyranny

This simple reversal of a value's charge from positive to negative is not, however, the limit of villainy. In a lawful society, the possibility of justice still exists. When a law is broken, crime fighters can restore it. But the profound violations of an extraordinary villain can take a value beyond its negative charge.

If a villain uses her vast wealth to corrupt society into a despotic realm, injustice blackens into tyranny. When the rule of law either no longer exists or cannot be enforced, this villain governs not by law but by an edict: *Might Makes Right*.

In the *Star Wars* universe, the force-wielding Dark Lords of the Sith embrace a triad of Machiavellianism, narcissism, and psychopathy. These grotesque kratocrats know no shame. They openly celebrate their brutality, making no pretense about who they are, what they want, and how they intend to get it.

4. Deception

The deadliest tactic of the most compelling villains is the weaponized lie. Characters who rely on brains rather than brawn or magic or mutation or time travel or any other superweapon are by far the most difficult to write. With or without a superpower, these villains use deception to outsmart the hero and lure her into a mercy scene. This turning point forces the writer to engineer her hero's escape by outsmarting her own villain's virtuoso scheme. This takes talent.

To finish our villain's story, suppose that once she gains absolute power over her institution, she does not behave like a despot. Instead, she masquerades as an honest leader and feigns devotion to justice. As a result, her lie-disguised tyranny turns believers into victims.

THE BEARING OF POWER

To complete a compelling villain, give thought to the way the character expresses herself in speech and gesture, in behavior and appearance.

Powerful people conserve energy. Tyrants own slaves; the rich hire servants. Those in command observe and analyze ongoing situations while others do what needs doing. People with secure power carry themselves with an air of someone who expects to have things done for them, while those with an insecure grip on power seem edgy and apprehensive.

In *Mission: Impossible—Ghost Protocol*, the IMF team desperately improvises, scrounging for transport and weapons, while Cobalt calmly strolls through events, getting everything he needs when he needs it.

In *Die Hard*, John McClane wildly hops barefoot through broken glass, berating himself, while Hans Gruber glides though the story, taking his time, musing about men's fashion.

The truly powerful never raise their voices, but when they speak, people listen. In Cecil B. DeMille's *The Crusades*, rulers from all over Europe confront Saladin, sultan of the Middle East, and loudly boast: "We do not fear you. We are many kings with one army." Saladin smiles quietly. "I am one king . . . with many armies."

In *Game of Thrones*, who was the greater threat to the Stark family: the frenetic Joffrey or his mother, the calm-spoken Cersei Lannister? The difference is the critical trait of characterization that separates a powerful personality from a cowardly neurotic: dignity.

Without dignity, heroes lose their moral authority; without dignity, villains lose their institutional authority. Even a villain who indulges in opulence and luxury can acquire a kind of ruthless dignity.

Consider Viggo, the villain in *John Wick*.

As a kid, Viggo fought his way out of the slums of Kiev and up the underworld food chain to become the head of the Tarasov crime family. John Wick once worked for Viggo as a hit man, and they developed a kind of father/son rapport, but then they became enemies when Iosef, Viggo's son, killed Daisy, John's dog.

Viggo is a charming ultra-bad guy. His dialogue mixes poetic imagery

THE BEARING OF POWER

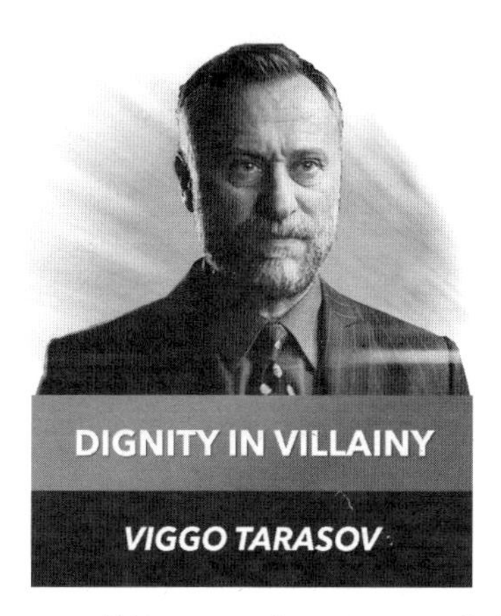

*Mixes **poetic imagery** with **gangster profanity**.*
***Sharp insights** counterpoint Wick's **blunt stoicism**.*

with gangster profanity. His quirky personality finds humor in hypervio-lence. His sharp insights counterpoint John Wick's blunt stoicism; Viggo's ironic smile frames his gangster dignity.

POWER IN THE SUBTEXT

Caped costumes, muscled bodybuilders, uniforms draped with medals suggest power but do not and cannot guarantee it. Power radiates from deep within a character. Audiences sense this instinctively.

TEXT: The sensory surface of a work of art. What strikes the eye, the ear. In sculpture, what we see. In music, what we hear. In story, the surface behaviors of what characters say and do.

SUBTEXT: The inner life of a work of art. In sculpture, the tension between mass and surface. In music, the emotional energy that pulses beneath sound. In story, the hidden conscious thoughts and suppressed emotions that flow below a character's words and deeds, as well as even deeper subconscious needs and drives.

As a cast member comes into view, audience members take clues from what they see and hear on the textual surface, then intuit the unspoken thoughts and feelings in the character's subtext, and with that insight, they sense the presence or absence of power. What's more, within the first few scenes, even before anyone takes a major action, storygoers perceive the cast's social hierarchy from bottom to top, least powerful to most powerful.

In Action, a hidden subtext adds danger to stillness. Building heat in the subtext while coolly underplaying threats on the surface intrigues an audience into looking deeply into the cast. A hint of the unspoken urges them to sense what is not being said or done visibly but happening nonetheless in the inner life.

Consider the opening scene of *Casino Royale*:

Beat #1

INT. SECTION CHIEF'S PRAGUE OFFICE—NIGHT

When the chief enters his office, he's startled to see his wall safe hanging open.

> **BOND:** *(hidden in the shadows)* M really doesn't mind you earning a little money on the side, Dryden. She'd just prefer if it weren't selling secrets.

SUBTEXT: CALLING THE CHIEF A TRAITOR.

As the chief calmly sits down, he stealthily opens his desk drawer, his gun inside.

SUBTEXT: PREPARING TO KILL BOND.

Beat #2

> **CHIEF:** Are the theatrics supposed to scare me? You have the wrong man, Bond. If M was so sure I was bent, she'd have sent a double-O.

SUBTEXT: BELITTLING BOND.

Bond stares calmly at the chief.

SUBTEXT: LEADING HIM ON.

Beat #3

CHIEF: *(cont'd)* Benefits of being section chief: I'd know if anyone had been promoted to double-O status. Wouldn't I?

SUBTEXT: BELITTLING BOND FOR THE SECOND TIME.

Bond smiles, his eyes on the target.

SUBTEXT: ENJOYING THE DUEL.

Beat #4

CHIEF: Your file shows no kills. And it takes . . .

SUBTEXT: BELITTLING BOND FOR THE THIRD TIME.

BOND: *(interrupting)* Two.

SUBTEXT: INTIMIDATING THE CHIEF.

Beat #5

FLASHBACK TO INT. PUBLIC LAVATORY—NIGHT
A tenacious but cool Bond fights a man hand-to-hand.

SUBTEXT: RAGING EMOTION AND IMPROVISATION.

Beat #6

INT. SECTION CHIEF'S OFFICE—SAME
The chief pulls his gun on Bond.

CHIEF: Shame. We barely got to know each other.

SUBTEXT: LORDING HIS POWER OVER BOND.

The chief pulls the trigger. The gun clicks. No bullets.

SUBTEXT: REVEALING BOND'S TRICK.

The chief stares at his gun.

SUBTEXT: COPING WITH THE SHOCK.

Beat #7

Bond holds up the gun's magazine clip.

> **BOND:** I know where you keep your gun. I suppose that's something.

SUBTEXT: TAUNTING THE CHIEF.

> **CHIEF:** True. How did he die?

SUBTEXT: BRACING FOR HIS FATE.

> **BOND:** Your contact? Not well.

SUBTEXT: SAVORING THE MOMENT.

Beat #8

FLASHBACK: INT. PUBLIC LAVATORY—SAME

Bond drowns his adversary in a sink, then stands over the body, regaining composure.

SUBTEXT: SUPPRESSING HIS EMOTIONS.

Beat #9

> **CHIEF:** Made you feel it, did he?

SUBTEXT: RESIGNING HIMSELF TO HIS FATE.

Bond continues staring.

SUBTEXT: GIVING THE CHIEF A LAST MOMENT.

Beat #10

> **CHIEF:** *(cont'd)* Well... you needn't worry. The second is...

SUBTEXT: GOING OUT WITH DIGNITY.

Before the chief can finish his sentence, Bond shoots and kills him.

> **BOND:** Yes. Considerably.

SUBTEXT: ENJOYING THE KILL.

Essentially, this is an assassination scene that makes the audience wonder, "When will the guns come out?" But by keeping the true thoughts and feelings of both Bond and the chief in the subtext, tension tightens, suspense peaks, and the lethal act hits with surprise.

PART 3

ACTION DESIGNS

Part Two concentrated on Action's three core roles to help you imagine your characters in full before they enter your story. Part Three takes the reverse angle. The next several chapters lay out what happens in an Action telling no matter who fills the roles. We detached character creation from event design to train you as a two-fisted artist before you step into the ring. The moment you hit the keyboard, however, the two never really separate.

In virtually every Action writer's experience, the creative process sends her talents back and forth between two poles of design: character and event. Fitting character to event and event to character fills the yin and yang of an author's day.

Characters cause events and events cause change. Beat by beat, an author, like a chemist, synthesizes two substances—human nature and the forces of change—into a third, new thing: story.

When a character's actions impact her world, the reaction she gets alters the balance of her life, moving her and the event she's in toward a more positive or more negative stage. If a scene's value charge stays the same from one end to the other, then nothing essentially changes, and therefore, nothing happens. Random chance aside, a scene without a character-caused turning point is a nonevent and probably boring.

Let's look at the design of events in Action.

8

THE INCITING INCIDENT

A person can cope with everyday annoyances so long as he feels he is ultimately in control of his life. He wants what we all want: sovereignty over existence.

An inciting incident launches a story by shattering that sense of sovereignty. This event radically impacts a protagonist's life, swinging a critical value out of balance from positive to negative (a wealthy man falls into poverty) or from negative to positive (an enslaved man escapes to freedom). This major turning point happens in only one of two ways: by choice or by coincidence.

For example: In a Crime Story, a criminal's premeditated choice to commit murder changes the balance of a detective's world from justice to injustice (positive to negative). In a Love Story, the random meeting of two lonely strangers that sparks an attraction changes the balance of their lives from isolation to intimacy (negative to positive).

When life swings out of balance, that disruption sparks the instinctive desire to restore equilibrium. We may at first be uncertain about what to do, but in time we imagine a rebalanced future, a change that would put life back on its feet. Sooner or later, a balanced future comes more and more into focus and centers on a specific purpose or *object of desire*.

A story's object of desire is defined as the thing or situation that the protagonist believes he needs to restore his life's balance. It could be a physical object he could hold in his hand: espionage secrets hidden in a thumb drive. Or it could be a change of relationship: marriage to a beloved in a Love Story or a unified family in a Domestic Drama. It could be a social objective: a victory that restores peace to a country or freedom to a population.

Do not confuse object of desire with motivation. An object of desire is what a protagonist wants; motivation is why he wants it. A sense of moral duty motivates James Bond in *Casino Royale*, revenge in *Quantum of Solace*, guilt in *Skyfall*, and all three combined in *Spectre*. These different motivations drive Bond toward the same object of desire: a dead villain. An Action hero's motivation is always unique to him and his story. What a character wants and why he wants it call for two separate but critical acts of writerly creativity.

In an Action Story, the hero's life spins fully out of balance to the negative with the discovery of three things:

1. The villain.
2. The villain's plan.
3. The MacGuffin the villain needs to execute that plan (more on MacGuffins in Chapter Ten).

These three discoveries propel the hero along a spine of action aimed at the defeat of the villain, the destruction of his plan, the rescue of the victim, and the restoration of security. All three elements could be discovered in a single face-to-face scene or split into three separate events. The discovery of any one element could begin the story.

James Bond spots Franz Oberhauser, the villain in *Spectre*, before he knows what Oberhauser wants, how he plans to get it, or how he will use it. *Guardians of the Galaxy* lifts off when Star-Lord Peter Quill steals the story's MacGuffin, a mysterious orb, even though he has no idea what powers and purposes hide within. Jack Bauer discovers a villain's plan in the first episode of every *24* season but not who he is or what he needs to carry it out his scheme.

Mission: Impossible—Ghost Protocol, a five-act film, spreads the inciting incident over its first two acts: An assassin opens Act One with the murder of an IMF agent and theft of secret documents to sell to Cobalt, a covert villain. But before Ethan Hunt's team can identify Cobalt, he blows up the Kremlin and pins its destruction on Hunt, climaxing Act One. The full inciting incident clicks in place at the Act Two climax when Ethan uncovers Cobalt and his plan to start World War III by striking San Francisco with a missile (the MacGuffin) launched from a Russian nuclear submarine.

Identifying villain, plan, and MacGuffin sends a hero into action, but any of these discoveries could be false: A faux villain might open a story, hiding the true villain who does not appear until midway into the telling (*The Dark Knight*); a villain, like Loki, might lie about his plan (*Thor: Ragnarok*); or he may deceive the hero with a false MacGuffin (*Die Hard*).

No matter how the three key discoveries are made, the hero may simply refuse to act. *Spider-Man*'s Peter Parker has portrayed the reluctant hero throughout his career, constantly questioning his decision to play the superhero. In fact, issue #50 of *The Amazing Spider-Man* comic book is titled "Spider-Man No More!"

As complex as Action storytelling can become, the inciting incident in most tellings is straightforward. In *Jaws*, for instance, a sheriff discovers the dismembered victim of a shark attack.

PLACEMENT OF THE INCITING INCIDENT

The principle that guides placement of the inciting incident is simple: Bring in the central plot's inciting incident as soon as possible, but not until it delivers its full impact.

From story to story, the inciting incident's ideal moment could happen anywhere from the first scene to the climax of the Act One—or in rare cases such as *Mission: Impossible—Ghost Protocol*, further on. The exact moment to launch a story depends on the amount of exposition necessary to set it up. If you bring the inciting incident in before the audience/reader sufficiently understands the situation, they may be confused; if you wait until long after they know all they need to know, they may lose interest.

On one hand, if the reader/audience needs no prior knowledge, the inciting incident can open the telling immediately, as it does in *Jaws*. If, on the other hand, the audience/reader needs an in-depth backgrounding in roles and context, time and place, the inciting incident might arrive much later.

In *Django Unchained*, for instance, the audience needs to understand the slavery-based culture of the American South of the 1850s and bounty hunting as a profession, along with the life histories of the two heroes, so it can react fully when Django wins his freedom by killing three white overseers thirty-nine minutes into the film.

As mentioned, the expositional load in *Ghost Protocol* is very complex, so the telling staggers the hero's three discoveries throughout the first two acts. The intricate logistics of the film's four-part MacGuffin, plus the identity of the villain and his plan, could not be front-loaded into a single exposition-packed opening scene for fear that critical elements might be overlooked or forgotten or cause confusion or simply bore the audience. Instead, by giving each expositional unit its own dramatized scene, the telling intrigues the audience, step by dynamic step, and then delivers the inciting incident with exciting force.

THE HERO AND VILLAIN MEET

With exceptions, action villains rarely know the hero prior to the inciting incident. This creates a writing problem: Because a hero can only go into action after he discovers the villain's plan, how to stage this encounter? The need to reveal an ongoing scheme to the hero often triggers ham-handed contrivances... unless the writer finds an honest motivation.

In *Die Hard*, for instance, Hans Gruber never heard of John McClane until the cop stumbles into the master thief's heist at the top of a skyscraper. McClane's coincidental discovery is motivated, however, because he was trying to discover something else: the whereabouts of his estranged wife.

Many heroes work in action services such as law enforcement or the military. These professions give characters a credible way to cross paths with a Life/Death situation while possessing the skills and capacities that allow them to survive and save other lives.

A hero's entrance into the story happens, as we've noted, in one of two ways: by coincidence or by choice. If by coincidence, the hero could be in the wrong place at the wrong time (*Gravity*) or the right place at the right time (*Star Wars: Episode IV—A New Hope*). If by choice, it could be the villain's choice to involve the hero (*The Dark Knight*) or the hero's choice to involve himself (*Casino Royale*). A third way combines the two: Coincidence trips the hero into trouble, but choice keeps him on track (*Die Hard*). Once in danger, the hero must then improvise tactics against the dark scheme of a powerful foe.

THE SET PIECE PROLOGUE

As audiences and readers settle into an Action Story, they naturally wonder, "Who is the hero and what can he do?" A set piece prologue, such as Indiana

Jones fleeing a massive boulder in the opening sequence of *Raiders of the Lost Ark* or James Bond killing two villains to ignite *Casino Royale*, answers these questions instantly, dramatizes the hero's powers, and hooks the audience's curiosity, preparing them for the inciting incident that follows.

Other tellings, however, create an aura of mystery around the hero and slowly reveal his dimensions and talents throughout the entire story.

THE SETUP SUBPLOT

If the central plot's inciting incident needs extensive exposition to set it up, Action tellings can prepare the ground by calling on a subplot to grab interest and dramatize that exposition.

Predator opens with an army special operations team led by Dutch Schaefer attacking a jungle encampment in South America, trying to rescue political prisoners held by Soviet-backed rebels. This subplot carries the first thirty-six minutes of the film, dramatizing the specialized skills of each member of Schaefer's team. Just as this subplot climaxes, an alien who hunts human beings for sport attacks and kills one of the team, igniting the central plot.

CROSSCUTTING HERO AND VILLAIN

Another technique to dramatize exposition while building to a delayed inciting incident opens the telling with crosscut scenes between the hero's point of view and the villain's point of view. The openings of *Die Hard*, *The Dark Knight*, and *Star Trek II: The Wrath of Khan* all edit back and forth between two subplots, one starring the hero, the other the villain, raising high tension as the gap between them closes, until they finally clash at the inciting incident.

The central plot's inciting incident typically occurs within the first 25 percent of the telling. If an audience waits beyond that time for the central plot to begin, they presume that the power of the inciting incident requires major preparation. So, no matter which technique a writer employs to hold interest while setting up an inciting incident, the reader/audience senses a major surprise in the making. Indeed, the longer they wait, the greater their anticipation.

The inciting incident of *The Wrath of Khan* arrives at the forty-five-minute mark, almost half of the way through the telling. The film opens with two crosscut subplots: In one, Kirk trains cadets on the aging *Enterprise* while he wrestles with a loss of meaning in his life. A second subplot dramatizes Khan's escape from a barren, lifeless planet. Khan hijacks a Federation starship and cripples the *Enterprise*, trapping Kirk and forcing him to surrender. The climaxing of the two subplots serves as the Act One climax, the central plot's inciting incident, and the mercy scene all in one major turning point. The whole of Act Two then becomes an extended mercy scene until Kirk, his life once again packed with meaningful action, finally outwits Khan and climaxes the spine of action.

9

THE SPINE OF ACTION

The *spine of action* traces the protagonist's story-long quest for her object of desire. In the Action Genre, the spine begins with the hero's reaction to the inciting incident and ends with her climactic final tactic. In between, her pursuit traces dynamic cycles of ever-escalating antagonism, turning point by turning point, putting her life in greater and greater jeopardy as she struggles to defeat the villain's plan.

THE VILLAIN'S PLAN

The dark energy that radiates from the villain's plan permeates events. This scheme, almost always a bit mysterious, keeps the villain one step ahead. If she were to abandon her plan, action would grind to a halt. With no one to save, nothing at risk, the hero would hit a wall of inaction.

The twists and turns of the villain's plan have five prerequisites: They must be rational, probable, dangerous, rewarding, and character-specific.

1. Rational

The villain's plan must make sense. If a villain lacks the brainpower to devise a logical strategy, she'll just trip over herself. Why would we need a hero?

The villain in *Die Hard with a Vengeance* devises a lucid scheme: He broadcasts over the radio that he intends to blow up a school in New York City but doesn't specify which one. This panics the city as the entire police force frantically tries to evacuate every school. With the police completely swamped, the villain steals billions in gold bullion from a bank vault on Wall Street—the one section of Manhattan that has no schools. (This scenario was so ingenious that the FBI questioned the screenwriter to see if he in fact planned to pull it off.)

2. Probable

The villain's plan need not be fail-proof, but it must have a high probability for success. If John McClane were not in his way, Hans Gruber would have killed the hostages in *Die Hard* and made off with tens of millions in bearer bonds. If Ethan Hunt hadn't won the climactic briefcase scramble in *Mission: Impossible—Ghost Protocol*, Cobalt would have triggered Armageddon.

Most important, the plan must be coincidence-proof. It does not need the right thing to be in the right place at the right time.

The villain in *Die Hard 5: A Good Day to Die Hard* faces trial in Russia. His prison escape plan calls for him to be kidnapped simultaneously by three separate entities—the CIA, a Russian gangster, and a crash-out team led by his daughter. What's more, the success of this plan depends on the failure of two of the three kidnapping plots. Villains plan for success and prepare for failure—not the other way around.

Then again, success lurking behind seeming failure has a long history. Tricking your enemy into escorting you through their defenses was an original idea thirty-two centuries ago when a Greek army left a massive wooden horse (packed with hidden warriors) as a gift to the city of Troy. In *The Dark Knight*, the Joker recycles Odysseus's ingenious device by hinging his plan on getting caught. Over the next two years, *The Dark Knight Rises*, *Skyfall*, *Star Trek into Darkness*, and *A Good Day to Die Hard* recycled this plot device into an ever-sillier cliché.

3. Dangerous

The audience weighs the value of a thing when they see what people are willing to risk for it. The villain's plan, therefore, must be not only convincing but also dangerous in proportion to its goal. The more the villain expects to win, the greater the risk he must take.

For the Joker to reduce Gotham to anarchy, he must rob a bank, rob the mob, escape the mob's revenge, and then kill the mobsters themselves, along with a judge and police commissioner.

Hans Gruber can't simply hack into the Nakatomi corporate computer and siphon its wealth. To steal his fortune, he must instead kidnap a building full of hostages, then masquerade as a terrorist so he can manipulate the FBI and city police.

4. Rewarding

What the villain wants must be extremely valuable, something that endows him with immense wealth or power or both. Otherwise, there's no reason to destroy lives to get it.

5. Character-Specific

The villain's plan mirrors his nature. Just as the hero's reaction to the villain's plan must be character-specific, so too the villain's plan.

Consider two narcissistic megalomaniacs: Ronan from *Guardians of the Galaxy* and Cobalt from *Mission: Impossible—Ghost Protocol* devise megalomaniacal plans to destroy civilization so they can re-create it and be worshipped for their godlike power. Ronan pursues this desire with a fanatical righteousness going back generations. Cobalt, in his twisted mind, thinks destroying the world will restart humanity and make him its guardian angel.

The invention of an Action Story, therefore, begins with the design of its villain, followed by a hero who reacts to this villainy with unique resources and tactics. So, to restate for emphasis: The villain's psychology and the schemes it invents drive the Action Plot; the hero's reactions to them propel its spine of action.

ROGUES IN A ROW

In franchises such as *Spider-Man* or long-form series such as *The Mandalorian*, the same protagonist faces a gallery of villains, each testing the hero in a one-off way. The most memorable villains bring out never-seen-before qualities in the hero.

The Joker tests Batman's cool under pressure; the Riddler's puzzles draw out his powers of deduction; Scarecrow challenges his courage; Catwoman seduces his morality; Bane measures his strength. So, whether a hero appears in one story or a hundred, each villain's powers and plans create a one-of-a-kind test only this villain could invent and an improvisational solution only this hero could imagine.

THE VILLAIN'S SECRET

The more transparent the villain's plan, the more predictable and threatless the villain. The more mysterious the villain's plan, the more menacing the villain and the more surprise-filled the spine of action.

In *Die Hard*, Hans Gruber has a secret: He is not a terrorist, he's a thief. In *The Empire Strikes Back*, the archvillain Darth Vader has a secret: He's the hero's father. Even nonhuman villains have secrets. After the plane crash that opens *The Grey*, a wolf pack encircles and growls at the surviving passengers, as if to drive them off their hunting territory. But eventually the survivors discover that in fact, from the beginning, the wolves have been herding them closer and closer to the pack's den.

The villain's secret must be more than a minor expositional fact such as his real name, his history behind bars, his abusive childhood. Instead, its revelation must impact events powerfully by building, progressing, and complicating conflict, spinning events in a new direction.

Contrast *Batman: Mask of the Phantasm* with *Batman Begins*. Both are Batman origin stories that chronicle how and why Bruce Wayne donned the cape and cowl. The villain in both possesses a secret identity.

In *Batman: Mask of the Phantasm*, a masked vigilante known as the Phantasm hunts down and executes Gotham's mob leaders one by one. Suspicion falls on Batman. As the police pursue him for these crimes, Bruce Wayne investigates the mystery and discovers a link to his past. Ten years prior, when he was in secret training to become a crime fighter, he met Carl Beaumont and his beautiful daughter, Andrea. He fell in love with Andrea, but then father and daughter suddenly vanished. Heartbroken, he donned Batman's cape for the first time.

Back in the present, Bruce discovers ties between the Phantasm's victims and Andrea's father, Carl. Carl invested money for the mob. But when he lost a fortune, the gangsters put a hit out on him. Carl took his daughter and fled to buy time. He soon dug up the money and paid the mob back with interest, but they killed him anyway.

As Bruce pieces clues together, he deduces the secret: The Phantasm is and has always been Andrea. Her assassinations of gangsters avenge her father's murder. Now Batman has a rather special problem.

In *Batman Begins*, a young Bruce Wayne studies combat skills, taught by his mentor Henri Ducard of the League of Shadows, a secret society of assassins led by Ra's al Ghul. Wayne ultimately refuses to join the league and escapes its stronghold during a fire, saving Ducard's life but leaving Ra's al Ghul to die.

Years later, Bruce Wayne as Batman pursues a villain scheming to poison Gotham City with a hallucinogenic toxin. Wayne discovers that the criminal mastermind is Ra's al Ghul. In the same way he masquerades as Batman, Henri Ducard masquerades as Ra's al Ghul. The man he saw die in the fire at the League of Shadows was a decoy. But this revelation has no effect on either the villain's plan or Batman's efforts to stop it. Their hero/villain dynamic continues; the secret was not worth keeping or discovering.

One last word about secrets: They generate curiosity, but once a secret's revelation spins a turning point, giving readers and audiences what they want to know, there should be no need for added exposition. A turning point followed by an explanation of how and why what just happened prompts a rewrite from page one.

ACTION PROGRESSION

When a hero takes an action designed to cause a positive reaction in her world, a turning point opens between what she thought would happen and what in fact happens. Negative forces, more powerful and different than she expected, erupt. This unforeseen impasse blocks her immediate goal and, with that, her long-term desire.

The instant this occurs, the audience/reader instinctively realizes that this is a *point of no return*. The action the hero just took did not get her what she wants. Therefore, there is no retreat. She cannot reuse this tactic or go back to strategies of lesser quality, magnitude, or risk. She must move forward to maneuvers that demand ever-greater brains, guts, and danger.

Turning points along a spine of action progress a story's conflicts by demanding greater and greater willpower from the hero, generating greater and greater jeopardy for the hero, passing points of no return in terms of the breadth, depth, and impact of her actions. The more a hero hopes to achieve, the rockier her road. (See *Story*, pages 208–210.)

To accelerate events, Action villains must evolve in strength. In *The Dark Knight*, the Joker begins as a thief but transforms into ruler of Gotham's underworld. In *X-Men: First Class*, the villain, Sebastian Shaw, has the power to absorb any attack thrown against him, which in turn makes him stronger. The harder he's hit, the harder he hits back. In the Action/Sci-Fi/Comedy *Evolution*, a microscopic life-form that feeds on fire lands on Earth. When the military napalms the microbe, it grows into a massive monstrosity.

Conflict in an Action Story progresses and deepens the more the villain gains leverage over the hero. Their clashes build excitement in one of four possible ways: The villain makes it personal, global, private, or invisible.

1. Making It Personal

Conflict progresses to the personal the moment a villain directs an attack against the hero's family, friends, or lovers. The hero/victim link often offers an easy target for this tactic. The more intimate the hero's relationship to the victim, the more high-risk actions the hero will take and the greater the sacrifices she will make. Consider, for instance, the blood-soaked, hands-in-the-air, feet-lacerated-with-glass-shards entrance of John McClane when he confronts the villain at the climax of *Die Hard*—all to save his wife.

The hero/villain conflict can also become personalized. *The Empire Strikes Back* pits father against son; the *X-Men* prequels turn the "frenemies" Charles Xavier and Magneto against each other.

In a twist on this design, the hero might make it personal for the villain, gaining advantage when the villain loses emotional control. The *Die Hard* franchise has replayed this device three times over: In *Die Hard*, John McClane kills Karl's brother, sending Karl over the edge. In *Die Hard with a Vengeance*, the villain, Simon Gruber, pursues McClane because he killed his brother Hans. In *Live Free or Die Hard*, McClane kills the villain's girlfriend; the villain returns the favor by kidnapping McClane's daughter.

2. Making It Global

Instead of turning inward, a telling could go wide and greatly expand its conflict to a global scale. If villains possess vast power, as do aliens in *Independence Day*, or victims have enormous reach, as does the US president in *Olympus Has Fallen*, then action scenes ramify like nuclear fission.

3. Making It Private

An ingenious villain turns the hero inward against herself. She could inflict her with grief by killing someone she loves (Drax the Destroyer in *Guardians of the Galaxy*) or with guilt by destroying something the hero tried to save (James T. Kirk in *Star Trek III: The Search for Spock*) or with doubt of her own powers (Neo in *Matrix*) or with any other self-destroying weapon the hero uses to punish herself.

4. Making It Invisible

In the same way that searching for something in the dark slows action to a crawl, hunting for the truth in a fog of deception turns a hero in circles. So, the cleverest villains hide behind lies, disguising greed as charity, hatred as love, evil as good. In nearly every Pixar film—*Up*, *Wall-E*, *Toy Story 3*—villains conceal cruelty behind a mask of kindness.

Die Hard opens with Hans Gruber's masquerade as he pretends to be a freedom fighter bargaining for the release of political prisoners. In *The Incredibles*, Syndrome not only cloaks his vileness as virtue but pretends to love a family of superheroes while secretly plotting to kill them one by one.

THE REACTIVE VILLAIN

Villains who defend their fortresses against attack may have a reactive role in the War Genre but not Action. To repeat for emphasis: The villain's execution of her plan drives the story outward; the hero's reaction to each villainous step generates her tactics down a spine of action that brings events to climax.

10

THE MACGUFFIN

Definition: A MacGuffin is the thing that both hero and villain want, and if either of them gets it, it gives him power over the other.

This term was coined in jest by screenwriter Angus MacPhail and popularized by Alfred Hitchcock. Thanks to MacPhail, *MacGuffin* gives us a memorable name for an essential component for all Action Stories.

VARIETY AND PROGRESSION

A MacGuffin may be physical, such as the falcon in *The Maltese Falcon*, the Blackwater heist money in *Red Dead Redemption II*, the One Ring in *Lord of the Rings*, or even the story's victim, such as the Child in *The Golden Child*.

A MacGuffin may be mental, perhaps a secret hiding in a character's mind. At the climax of *The 39 Steps*, a music hall performer, Mr. Memory, recites by rote the MacGuffin, an extraordinarily long numerical code for a top-secret aircraft engine. Or it may be virtual, such as the glowing globe known as the Easter Egg in *Ready Player One*.

Genres such as Crime, Sci-Fi, and Political Drama often use a piece of information as MacGuffin: the plans that show a weakness in the Death Star in *Star Wars*; evidence of corruption by the head of the NSA in *Enemy of the State*; the hiding place of US embassy officials in *Argo*. These diplomats are safe so long as their whereabouts in Tehran stays secret, but should the Iranian government discover this MacGuffin, the staff will be captured and executed.

Typically, the Action Genre's MacGuffin is a single thing such as the intelligence-sharing global network code-named Nine Eyes in *Spectre*.

Occasionally, a number of objects combine into a MacGuffin: In *Mission: Impossible—Ghost Protocol*, the villain gains control of a nuclear missile by stringing together a combination of launch codes, launch devices, a nuclear submarine, and a missile.

No matter how it's characterized, a MacGuffin focuses the actions of both hero and villain and measures their success—whoever controls the MacGuffin controls the outcome.

In some tellings, the protagonist's object of desire and the story's MacGuffin coincide as the victim becomes the MacGuffin and his rescue the hero's object of desire. In other tales, the MacGuffin gives the hero the means to rescue the victim.

In *Casablanca*, Rick Blaine's object of desire is Ilsa Lund, the woman he loves, but to rescue her, he needs one of the most famous MacGuffins in the history of the cinema, a Letter of Transit—an unquestionable, unrescindable, invaluable MacGuffin that frees anyone who holds one.

MacGuffins grant power. In *The Lord of the Rings*, if Sauron possesses the One Ring, he will use it to conquer the free peoples of Middle-Earth. The hero's job, therefore, is to keep the MacGuffin out of the villain's hands, even if he doesn't understand its full nature. In *Raiders of the Lost Ark*, Indiana Jones wants to save the Ark for its archaeological value, all the while unaware of its supernatural powers.

The strongest MacGuffins are variable, progressive, and portable.

Variable: The repetitiousness of chase, chase, chase, chase, fight, fight, fight, fight may be the thorniest problem the action writer ever faces. An effective MacGuffin inspires a variety of tactical actions/reactions from hero and villain that never repeat.

Progressive: No matter the surface activity in scenes, diminishing stalemates with less and less conflict, less and less threat to life feel equally repetitious. Again, the MacGuffin must help drive the turning points in an ever-rising progression of danger.

Portable: To increase variety of action and progression of risk, the MacGuffin often needs to move, to be lost and found, hidden and discovered, stolen and traded.

To build these diverse, ever-rising, ever-changing conflicts, hero and villain can interact with the MacGuffin in one of three ways:

1. Both hero and villain seek the MacGuffin. In *Raiders of the Lost Ark*, the Nazis and Indiana Jones scour the desert for the Ark of the Covenant.
2. The hero hides the MacGuffin from the villain. In *The Lord of the Rings*, Frodo struggles to conceal and destroy the One Ring before Sauron can find it and use it.
3. The hero steals the MacGuffin from the villain. In *Mission: Impossible—Ghost Protocol*, the IMF team captures Cobalt's devices, piece by piece, as he launches a nuclear rocket at the US.

THE MACGUFFIN IN ACTION

The MacGuffin holds the key to the villain's plan, and with that life and death for the victim, so the audience expects that at some point the MacGuffin will be demonstrated or at least described. Keeping the MacGuffin hidden may work in a Murder Mystery, but in Action, story-long secrecy dulls excitement.

The introduction of the MacGuffin can happen anywhere in the telling, even before the inciting incident. In the opening sequence of *The Golden Child*, the Child demonstrates his supernatural powers by bringing a dead bird back to life. He's soon kidnapped, becoming both victim and MacGuffin.

Fast & Furious 9 opens with a subplot that takes place thirty years in the past. It dramatizes Dom's suspicion that his brother Jakob killed their father. This lays the groundwork for the central plot's inciting incident when, decades later, Jakob robs Dom of the film's MacGuffin, a computer hacking device.

The MacGuffin need not be fully exposed from the onset. In fact, giving the reader/audience only what they need to know to follow the story while holding back some elements can create tension around the MacGuffin that delivers eye-popping revelations later in the telling.

In *Men in Black*, intragalactic war hangs in the balance as two heroes and a villain chase after a MacGuffin said to be on "Orion's belt." The heroes try to connect it to the constellation Orion, only to finally discover that it's a bobble dangling from a collar belted around the neck of a cat named Orion.

When the Action Genre merges with a subgenre, such as Espionage, a mystery MacGuffin adds intrigue to excitement. As the title suggests, the MacGuffin in *The Bourne Identity* is the identity of the amnesic Jason Bourne. The CIA knows who he is, but Bourne must sleuth his way to uncovering the secret. Bit by bit, Bourne exposes not only his identity but also Treadstone, a CIA black ops scheme, gutting its power.

In *North by Northwest*, traitors steal the MacGuffin, a top US secret, and hide it on a spool of microfilm. They intend to sell the microfilm and whatever is on it to a foreign enemy, but the screenplay never reveals exactly what that secret is. Instead, screenwriter Ernest Lehman leaves it to the audience's imagination, knowing the deadly weapon they imagine will be more catastrophic than anything he could invent.

The scene-by-scene drive of the spine of action ultimately depends on the MacGuffin. Without a MacGuffin to focus conflicts, Action storytelling often dissolves into empty, superficial chases and shoot-outs, intercut with undramatized exposition that must constantly remind the audience of how much danger the characters are in. Sooner or later, and probably sooner, people toss the book or reach for the remote.

THE BRINK OF SUCCESS

Although a MacGuffin may be cloaked in intrigue, at some point it will reveal its power. The more control the villain has over the MacGuffin, the greater the danger for hero and victim. The greater the danger, the more intense excitement becomes, as the villain reaches the very brink of triumph.

Two examples:

The Fourth Act of *Mission: Impossible—Ghost Protocol* climaxes with the villain, Cobalt, launching a nuclear missile at San Francisco. The Fifth Act throws the IMF team into a desperate scramble to destroy the MacGuffin while it's still in the air.

The first two acts of *Guardians of the Galaxy* set up the crisis and climax as Ronan captures the Infinity Stone and implants it inside his hammer. He merely needs to strike the surface of Xandar to destroy the entire planet. As he raises his hammer, the Guardians have only the instant it takes for him to strike to save twelve billion Xandarians.

COMPLEX MACGUFFINS

Simple MacGuffins risk repetition; complex MacGuffins risk confusion; multiple MacGuffins risk splintering the plot.

A MacGuffin that swings back and forth from villain to hero to villain and back again may drag action into retrogressive chases, fights, and scrambles that echo and repeat.

Multipart MacGuffins may result in boring exposition dumps—scenes of underlings asking leading questions about how a MacGuffin's pieces fit together or, even worse, pace-killing lectures complete with slide projections that explain hows and whys of multiple MacGuffins.

On the other hand, the four-step MacGuffin of codes, launch device, communications satellite, and nuclear missile in *Mission: Impossible—Ghost Protocol* flows into a rich mix of action-filled scenes. The ultimate difference between what works and what doesn't begins with knowing the pitfalls and turning them to your advantage.

THE MACGUFFIN IN LONG FORM

One MacGuffin, with or without parts, may meet the demands of a two-hour feature film or standard-length novel, but the arc of long-form television or a series of linked novels calls for a MacGuffin that will sustain years of interest. Here are four possible solutions to the long-form problem: episodic MacGuffins, multiple MacGuffins, uber-MacGuffins, and characters-as-MacGuffin.

1. Episodic MacGuffins

Most Action series are episodic. Novel after novel, film after film, comic after comic, new story lines inspire new villainies with new MacGuffins. Heroes such as James Bond, Batman, Jason Bourne, Wonder Woman, Spider-Man, Ethan Hunt, and Dominic Toretto work their way through a gallery of rogues, each with a secret plan and hidden power—each episode inspiring a new MacGuffin.

2. Multiple MacGuffins

Consider the Action/Fantasy *Harry Potter.* Over her series of seven novels, J. K. Rowling developed three separate MacGuffins with a total of eleven parts: (1) the seven Horcruxes that contain the villain's soul; (2) the three Deathly Hallows of an Invisibility Cloak, Elder Wand, and Resurrection Stone; (3) Harry Potter himself.

Readers, as they slowly turn pages, can keep track of this dense complication, going back to reread or using margin notes when necessary. No film audience, however, could keep track of an eleven-part MacGuffin. The moviegoers who followed the Potter plotting without confusion most likely read the books before the screenings.

3. Uber-MacGuffins

A long-form television series such as *24* plays two dozen episodes per season, over multiple seasons, until it's bingeable for weeks on end. Long-form prose, such as *A Song of Ice and Fire* by George R. R. Martin, may take decades to write and months to read. Works of enormous magnitude magnify the twin problems of variety and progression exponentially. To solve these problems, long-form Action demands an uber-MacGuffin with uber-staying-power.

To achieve a richness of variety and progression, Marvel Studios invented the Infinity Stones, one grand MacGuffin composed of six sub-MacGuffins, each hidden inside a strange object and designed to motivate half a dozen distinctive films.

In *Captain America: The First Avenger,* the Space Stone hides inside a cosmic cube called the Tesseract that Captain America wrestles away from the Red Skull.

In *The Avengers,* the Mind Stone embeds inside Loki's mind-control scepter.

In *Thor: The Dark World,* the Reality Stone is in a liquefied form that could dissolve the universe into eternal darkness.

In *Guardians of the Galaxy,* the Collector acquires the orb that houses the Power Stone.

In *Doctor Strange,* Stephen Strange moves through time thanks to the Time Stone concealed in the Eye of Agamotto.

In the sixth episode, *Avengers: Infinity War,* the archvillain Thanos sacrifices his daughter so he can unite five Infinity Stones with the sixth, the Soul Stone. He then releases their combined cosmic power and destroys half of all life in the universe.

The three volumes of J. R. R. Tolkien's *The Lord of the Rings* take place during an epic War Story crosscut with supporting genres that encompass a vast cast and the entirety of his fantasy setting, Middle-Earth. But he kept the MacGuffin simple: the One Ring.

To create variety of action and progression of conflict, he gave the One Ring multiple powers: Anyone who wears it gains invisibility and immortality, yet at the same time becomes physically corrupted and wraith-like. He devised nineteen other Rings of Power, but the One Ring has power over them all.

4. Characters-as-MacGuffin

Because possession of a MacGuffin determines who lives and who dies, villains seek it to complete their plan, while heroes pursue it to prevent the villain's success. A MacGuffin, therefore, could be anything, including any of Action's core characters.

Hero-as-MacGuffin

A missile component or piece of government information is static and subject to repetition. A multidimensional hero solves this problem by engaging the audience emotionally and granting longevity to a story's spine of action.

Three heroes-as-MacGuffin:

In *The Matrix*, should Agent Smith kill Neo, the MacGuffin, the human rebellion will end, but should Morpheus save Neo, The One, and coach his powers, Neo will save humanity from the machines. Meanwhile, Neo searches constantly for belief in himself, his sense of what's true, what's false.

Throughout the Bourne trilogy—*Bourne Identity, Bourne Supremacy, Bourne Ultimatum*—Jason Bourne plays MacGuffin. Three villainous CIA chiefs struggle to control him because he possesses the power to quash their deadly schemes. Throughout this three-film span, however, Jason wrestles with amnesia, searching for his past, until it finally resurfaces at the climax of the trilogy.

Both *Star Wars* trilogies use the hero-as-MacGuffin. In the prequel, Anakin Skywalker fills that convention; in the original, Luke Skywalker plays MacGuffin. If Luke gives in to his anger and surrenders to the dark side, as did Anakin, a galaxy of victims will perish. In both trilogies, the Emperor seeks to control the galaxy by controlling Skywalker.

Victim-as-MacGuffin

In *Terminator 2: Judgment Day*, John Connor, a hero who duels AI villainy in the future, cannot protect his childhood self from the villain's time-traveling assassin. So, as a boy, he becomes both victim and MacGuffin.

In the long-form series *The Mandalorian*, Grogu (aka Baby Yoda) is a mysterious being with yet-to-be-realized telekinetic powers. Din Djarin, the hero, defends this victim-MacGuffin against every up-to-no-good villain in the universe.

Villain-as-MacGuffin

The villain-as-MacGuffin raises this problem: Giving the villain supreme power over life and death makes him far more deadly and exciting, but if he's supremely lethal, destroying him may seem improbable and unconvincing.

The MacGuffin in *Jaws* is a great white shark, a villain who's overwhelmingly powerful in his domain. For this reason, the hero's victory required a helpful coincidence. As the shark attacks, he accidentally lodges an explosive barrel in his jaws, making it conveniently easy for the sheriff to blow him up. Endings that need a bit of luck to turn positive are rarely as satisfying as those wholly in the hero's hands. *Jaws* seemed the exception.

Hero-Victim-Villain as MacGuffin

Action's three core roles can be combined, separated, and evolved in countless ways.

The Hulk and King Kong play all three roles and become a MacGuffin, too. They wield power over life and death, all the while wrestling with the consequences of their actions, the guilt that inflicts, and the likelihood of destroying others and themselves in the future.

In *The Dark Knight*, Harvey Dent begins as a co-hero with Batman, but the Joker kidnaps Dent and uses him as victim-MacGuffin in his "Gotham's soul" gambit. Finally, the Joker blows away half of Dent's face, turning him into the villain known as Two-Face. Harvey Dent moves from hero to victim to MacGuffin to villain.

The Hero-as-MacGuffin Problem

In many of the plot tactics listed earlier, it's possible that the hero will at some point either possess the MacGuffin or become the MacGuffin. In that moment, a story risks credibility: If the hero possesses the MacGuffin's power either as an object or within himself, why not use its power to destroy the villain? Or, if the story's logic will not allow that, why not destroy the MacGuffin so the villain cannot use it or, if necessary, sacrifice himself?

The novelist J. R. R. Tolkien found a satisfying answer: In his epic High Fantasy *The Lord of the Rings*, the MacGuffin, the One Ring, corrupts all who use it, turning them into the very kind of villain they want to defeat. The One Ring was forged in the fires of Mount Doom, and so it seems indestructible, but it is not. Those same fires could melt it down to nothing.

In the film trilogy of *The Lord of the Rings*, the hero, Frodo Baggins, gains possession of the all-powerful MacGuffin early in the telling. He knows he must destroy it but is constantly tempted to use its powers. This moral dilemma climaxes the epic: Standing on the edge of Mount Doom, Frodo must choose: Will he throw the One Ring into the volcano or give in to its seductive whispers? He chooses to keep the One Ring.

Suddenly, Gollum attacks, biting off Frodo's finger and snatching the One Ring. But while gleefully celebrating, Gollum loses his balance and falls into the volcano, incinerating himself and vaporizing the MacGuffin, ending the epic on a bit of *deus ex mishap*.

The MacGuffin may or may not be the hero's object of desire, but in all cases, it's the key to success.

11

TACTICS

Hero, as an idea, spans a spectrum from the virtually powerless (*127 Hours*) to the near omniscient (*Superman*). *Villain* covers the gamut of antagonists from the indifferent sea (*All Is Lost*) to an alien invasion (*Independence Day*). *Victim* encompasses all of humanity.

As diverse as these roles have become, their core desires never change over time: Villains want power; victims want rescue; heroes want to save victims from villains. What makes a character unique, however, is the specific strategy she uses to achieve her desire. Originality in role design, therefore, lies in *Action tactics*, the one-of-a-kind techniques characters employ to achieve their goals.

Harry Potter casts spells; Batman intimidates; James Bond kills. In *X-Men*, Cyclops projects laser beams, Wolverine grows claws, Xavier controls minds, Magneto controls metal. In *All Is Lost*, an unnamed yachtsman uses his seafaring know-how. While heroes always possess skill and power to some degree, the capacities of the villain they face always exceed them. Heroes try; villains succeed.

THE PRINCIPLE OF TACTICAL IMBALANCE

Principle: Villains are immune to the primary tactic of the hero; heroes have no defense against the primary strategy of the villain.

TACTICS

The two most common threats to a hero are the villain's secret plan and the juggernaut of time.

When a hero learns that a massively destructive, secretly devised scheme, created by an unknown villain, is running on a covertly calculated step-by-step timetable somewhere in the world, a flood of unanswered questions sweeps over that hero: Who is the villain? Where is she? What is her plan? When will it happen? The hero's vulnerability caused by this wave of unknowns is then doubled up by an unstoppable force: the onrush of time. The hero's race against time is her ultimate vulnerability. (See Chapter Twenty.)

These two vulnerabilities have driven the *Mission Impossible* franchise since its inception. In *Ghost Protocol* and *Fallout*, two recent examples, Ethan Hunt and his IMF team run from behind, trying to decipher the lunatic plans of anarchist madmen before they detonate nuclear weapons on to-the-second deadlines.

THE KILLER-HERO PROBLEM

If a hero's tactics make her overwhelmingly lethal, what immunity can protect a villain? Writers of speculative fiction solve this problem by designing physically unkillable villains, but the heroes of realistic action don't fight immortals or superpowered monsters. James Bond's chief weapon is a Walther PPK. A bullet from it would kill any Bond villain. So, what is the writer to do? Answer: Change the rules of engagement.

Bond has a license to kill... but only in self-defense.

In *Casino Royale*, Bond's portfolio is to uncover Le Chiffre's shadowy scheme, capture him alive, and bring him to M. This mission has driven his pursuit of every villain he ever faced from Goldfinger, Silva, and Mr. Greene to Blofeld, Trevelyan, and Sanchez. Bond is, after all, a spy, not an assassin. This elegant tactic has motivated over two dozen films.

Failure to solve the killer-hero problem leads to one of the most common failings of Action realism. In martial arts films, for instance, the rules of engagement cannot be changed. As a result, they typically create immunity in their villains with only one of two tactics: (1) superior knowledge of martial arts, and (2) an army of henchmen.

In the villain's first choice, the hero, faced with superior knowledge of a martial art, must find a new strategy or perfect an old one. Both relatively easy tasks. In the second choice, the villain tries to make up in quantity what she lacks in quality, but the hero usually just hacks her way through the gang, slaying henchmen two at a time. These overdog heroes force martial arts filmmakers to exploit the visual energy of martial artistry and shoot overlong scenes, substituting kinetic choreography for suspense-driven excitement.

A story setup, on the other hand, that takes away the hero's favorite tactic, while giving the villain an impenetrable immunity, presents an exciting tactical puzzle: How can the hero stop the unstoppable without her best weapon? The best Action writers create an undefeatable opponent, then take the hero's point of view and try to outsmart themselves.

THE ACHILLES' HEEL PROBLEM

An underdog who outsmarts or overpowers an overdog, using a tactic rooted in her character and executed without contrivance, is far and away the most difficult, thus most creative, test of the Action writer. Because so many stories fall short of this standard, Action has an Achilles' heel problem.

With the advent of Superman in 1938, the rise of superheroes inspired supervillains, making the problem of vulnerability versus immunity super as well, especially in the presentational genre of Fantasy. Many fantasy villains have absolute power over life and death. How can a hero penetrate this immunity? To solve the impasse, some writers resort to Homer's solution and inflict their villains with an Achilles' heel, a hidden fatal flaw.

This tactic creates a no-win dilemma for the writer: If a villain's Achilles' heel suddenly appears at the climax and saves the hero, the storyteller commits the genre's most egregious crime—the *deus ex machina* ending.

On the other hand, if a writer plants a fatal flaw in a villain early in the telling and the storygoer spots it, as sooner or later she will, she waits impatiently and wishes for somebody to throw the villain's off-switch. When someone finally does, she sits back annoyed because she saw it coming.

The easier and sooner an audience knows the answer to "How will this turn out?," the less and less satisfying the story.

Compare two villains who breathe through masks: Bane in *The Dark Knight Rises* and Darth Vader in *Star Wars*.

As soon as the audience discovers that Bane absorbs a lifesaving painkiller through his mask, the climax becomes obvious: Batman will fight Bane, rip off Bane's mask, put him in deadly agony, and finally win. To cast doubt on that outcome, the telling staged a previous fight during which Batman hit Bane's mask and nothing happened, but the storygoers were not fooled. They know an on-the-nose setup when they see one, especially if it's literally on a nose.

Imagine how exciting the climax to *The Dark Knight Rises* could have been if we discovered that Bane's mask, like Batman's cape, is a symbolic disguise or Bane's homage to Darth Vader. How would Batman defeat Bane then?

Darth Vader cannot breathe without his mask, but the audience does not learn this until the resolution scene in *Return of the Jedi*. After the mortally wounded Darth Vader kills the Emperor Palpatine, he asks Luke to take off his mask. Luke protests, saying he will die without it. That is the first and only mention that Darth Vader needed his mask to live. He had no Achilles' heel . . . that we knew of.

Great villains—Hans Gruber, Agent Smith, Jaws, the Joker, the Predator, the Alien, Henry Drax—have no built-in weaknesses.

An unflawed villain forces the writer to look inside the role for traits we never see coming—but once revealed, we realize were always there. These traits may seem like powers at first but then become weaknesses when the hero discovers how to use them to her advantage. No easy trick for hero or writer.

A weak villain begets a weak hero, and together they beget a weak story. Just as the great challenge of the Crime Genre is solving the perfect crime, the great challenge of Action is beating an invulnerable villain.

THE OMNIPOTENCE PROBLEM

If giving a villain enormous power drives a successful story, why not give him unlimited power?

Compare the T-1000 of *Terminator 2* with the T-X of *Terminator 3*. In both films, a shapeshifter pursues the heroes in a car.

In *Terminator 2*, the T-1000 cannot create weaponry greater than the mass of its liquid metal body. So, when Sarah Connor, her son John, and the T-800 flee in a stolen cop car, the T-1000 commandeers a car and gives chase. As it draws close, it transforms its hands into hooks, then dives forward and pierces the trunk of Connor's car. Pulling itself up, hook by hook, it smashes in the rear window, reaching for the kill. The T-800, armed with a shotgun, knows pellets can't kill the T-1000, so he fires at the quarter panel that holds the hooks. The metal tears away and T-1000 sails off into the street as Connor speeds away.

In *Terminator 3*, John Connor faces the T-X, a shapeshifter without limitations. It makes cannons from its hands. When it pursues Connor in the car chase, it climbs onto the car, turns its hand into a chain saw, and then carves into the rooftop. Its mission is to kill Connor, so, one wonders, why not re-create the massive gun it used in the previous scene and kill Connor instantly? Instead, the time it takes to cut a hole through the car roof gives Connor a chance to escape.

The T-1000's limitations inspire ingenuity; the unlimited T-X seems strangely dim-witted and incompetent.

The same problem arises in an overdog hero. Compare Superman with Green Lantern in the task of rescuing a helicopter.

In *Superman: The Movie*, a helicopter teeters off the edge of a skyscraper, Lois Lane trapped inside. As it plummets, Lois falls out. Superman flies up, grabs Lois with one hand and catches the falling helicopter with the other, then calmly puts them both back on the helipad. Superman is intelligent and compassionate.

In *Green Lantern*, Green Lantern possesses an alien ring that can construct anything he imagines by turning light into physical objects. So, when a helicopter spins out of control and threatens a society party atop a skyscraper, how does Green Lantern save the guests? He surrounds the helicopter with a Hot Wheels chassis, engines revving, tires spinning. He then builds a giant motor track around the rooftop and races the contraption in circles until it finally comes to a halt. Why not, one wonders, just land the helicopter? Or surround it with a barrier? His over-the-top solution makes Green Lantern seem reckless and childish.

When a hero or villain knows no limit, no matter what action she takes, an audience can always imagine something she hasn't done—something more sensical or more wonderful or simply more surprising.

THE DOPPELGÄNGER PROBLEM

In another solution to the omnipotence problem, hero and villain become mirror opposites with the same powers: Captain America fights the Red Skull, his evil twin; Iron Man fights Obadiah Stane in an updated smart suit; Hulk fights the Abomination, another gamma-irradiated monster; Superman fights General Zod, a fellow Kryptonian; Indiana Jones duels René Belloq, his rival archaeologist; the IMF chases the Syndicate, a corrupted version of itself; Batman and Bane both wear fearsome masks. And on go the duplications.

The villain-as-doppelgänger device often works, but just as often it worsens the very problem it intends to solve: A clone turns the underdog versus overdog duel into a dog-eat-dog stalemate. Stalemates lack that combination of fascination, mystery, and dread that fills an Action Story with menacing suspense. Instead, boredom swallows excitement as doppelgänger villains become predictable and unsurprising.

THE MERGER PROBLEM

What happens to the overdog/underdog dynamic when a character is both hero and villain? In most cases, an inner war rages until one psyche finally dominates the other. A couple of examples:

X-Men: First Class: Magneto arcs from hero to villain. He begins the story as an Auschwitz refugee and member of Charles Xavier's heroic ensemble of mutants who hunt the ex-Nazi Sebastian Shaw. But after Magneto kills Shaw, he becomes, like Shaw, an exclusivist who regards mutants as superior to human beings. He believes coexistence is impossible and so wants to replace Earth's dominant but archaic species with evolution's new breed of mutants.

Looper: Young Joe and Old Joe, time-traveling co-protagonists, arc in the opposite directions. Young Joe, a ruthless hired killer, meets his future self, Old Joe, a hero on a mission, and discovers that a telepathic psychopath will murder his wife and countless others in ten years' time. At climax, both Joes sacrifice themselves to blunt that future evil.

THE MONSTER PROBLEM

In Action, the power dynamic of hero and villain traps a victim in the middle. For Action's narcissistic villains, abusing others is the means to what they want. In Horror, the power dynamic eliminates the hero and pits a victim against a monster. For Horror's sadistic villains, abusing others gives them what they want. When the two genres merge, as in *Aliens* and *Predator*, the cast dynamic becomes hero-victim versus monster.

A monster comes from either an uncanny realm (a scientifically explainable but unimaginable phenomenon) or a supernatural domain (an imaginable but anti-scientific phenomenon). The best of Horror keeps the audience/reader guessing which is which.

In *The Shining*, Jack Torrance, the protagonist, becomes a murderous lunatic. But why? Are demonic hotel ghosts driving him mad or is he suffering from guilt, booze, and writer's block?

To protect herself, Jack's wife locks him in a pantry. He stands there, looking at the door, talking to a ghostly voice who chastises him for not killing his family. When Jack asks the voice for another chance, the door just . . . opens.

The audience has a choice of what made this protagonist a monster—madness or demons. Your guess is as good as mine, but whether this tale is uncanny or supernatural, it's Horror, not Action.

THE WHY-DOESN'T-SHE-JUST-KILL-HIM-WHEN-SHE-HAS-THE-CHANCE? PROBLEM

In the best Action writing, that question is never asked because the telling seems grounded and credible. If you create a fascinating and all-powerful villain, a courageous yet underdog hero, and give both thoroughly believable actions, the audience never doubts motivation. Every turning point will challenge the hero to survive and the villain to win. Well-dramatized scenes go unquestioned.

The problem, however, arises in mercy scenes when writers choose the I-want-you-to-suffer-horribly-before-you-die-but-I-can't-be-bothered-to-watch solution.

Batman Begins: As stately Wayne Manor, engulfed in flames, collapses around Batman, a wooden beam crashes down, trapping him. Ra's al Ghul, his archnemesis, looks down on the helpless Batman, but instead of killing him, Ra's shrugs and leaves him to die. Batman, of course, does not die. His butler, *deus ex Alfred*, serves him a silver-plated rescue.

In *Black Panther*, Killmonger (N'Jadaka) challenges Black Panther (T'Challa) to ritual combat for the throne of Wakanda. The villain wins the duel, but then, with the hero at his mercy, Killmonger chooses not to kill Black Panther on the spot and end any future threat. Instead, he throws him over a waterfall. Like so many heroes before him (Butch and Sundance, Richard Kimble, Sherlock Holmes), Black Panther survives, saved by *deus ex guy who owes the hero a favor.*

In *Superman: The Movie*, Lex Luthor tricks Superman into opening a box filled with kryptonite, hangs the glowing green mineral around Superman's neck, and nonchalantly pushes him into a swimming pool to drown. With Superman at the mercy of his superior intellect, Lex Luthor, a narcissist, takes pleasure in the idea of Superman dying a slow death but leaves before it happens because he's on a tight schedule.

He has launched two nuclear rockets in opposite directions: one aimed at California, the other at New Jersey. Even if Superman were to escape, he can't be in two places at the same time. Eve Teschmacher, wanting to save her Hackensack mother from nuclear evaporation, rescues Superman, who in turn saves New Jersey as a favor to Eve. In none of these three films does the hero outwit or outmuscle the villain.

Absent one of these two means, faux mercy scenes falsify jeopardy and fail to motivate the villain to pull the trigger. When death traps and mercy scenes work, they challenge the depths of courage and capacity in the hero. Essentially, a well-designed power dynamic turns an entire Action Story into one gigantic death trap.

As we laid out in Chapter Four, Action's core event, the mercy scene, calls for the hero to outsmart and/or outmuscle the villain. Of the two, outsmarting seems the more exciting and satisfying tactic. Four examples:

In *Mission: Impossible—Rogue Nation*, the IMF team outsmarts Solomon Lane in a judo-like move by using his rage to kill Ethan to propel him into a bulletproof Plexiglas trap.

In the mercy scene of *Guardians of the Galaxy*, Peter Quill breaks into a song-and-dance act that mystifies Ronan. Quill then grabs the Power Stone (one of the six Infinity Stones) from the distracted villain and all four Guardians absorb the stone's power, blasting Ronan out of existence.

At the *Die Hard* crisis, the villain has both the hero and the hero's wife at his mercy. McClane dupes Gruber into thinking he's unarmed, then diverts him by bursting into laughter, and finally drops him off a skyscraper.

In *The Wrath of Khan*, Spock analyzes Khan's battle tactics and deduces that he is inexperienced in three-dimensional combat. Kirk exploits this weakness and defeats the superhuman villain.

LIMITS

The reason why a particular villain is immune to a particular hero would not protect him from another hero; the reason why a particular hero is vulnerable to a particular villain would never work with other villains. The interplay between a specific hero and a specific villain is limited to them and would not succeed even in a sequel. The many distinctive duels between Batman and the Joker, as seen in comic book, animation, and on-screen, attest to that.

So be specific: Make certain that the tactics of your hero and villain become so mutually entwined that their interaction is not interchangeable with any other hero/villain or transferable to any other story.

12

SET PIECES

Set pieces are the arias of Action Stories. Their scenes turn the most powerful events and express the deepest truths of heroism and villainy. Never dismiss them as just fights or explosions. Audiences and readers, in fact, tend to judge a telling by the set pieces that drive its action sequences.

KEY TERMS

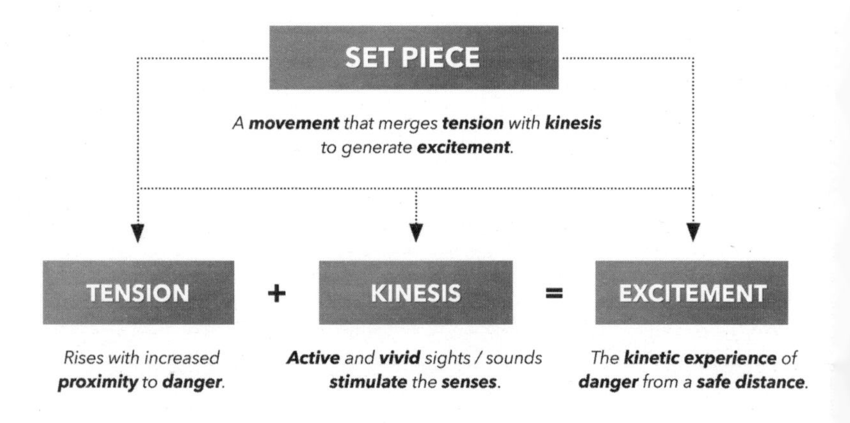

Set piece: A movement that merges *tension* and *kinesis* to generate *excitement*.

Tension: Proximity to danger—the closer and more extreme the danger, the greater the tension.
Kinesis: Stimulation of the senses—the more active and vivid the sights and sounds, the greater the energy, the greater the fun.
Excitement: The volatile experience of danger from a nonthreatening distance.

FROM TENSION TO KINESIS

A set piece could begin in edgy stillness. The high suspense of tension then slowly segues into flashing images and sudden sounds, building kinetic excitement.

In the opening of *Raiders of the Lost Ark*, enormous tension pulses as Indiana Jones slips into a decrepit catacomb, slowly evading death trap after death trap, inching nearer and nearer to a precious statue atop a pressure plate. To trick the plate, he switches a bag of sand for the statue. But the bag, too heavy, sinks the plate, and suddenly from overhead a huge boulder barrels toward him. Kinesis explodes as Indy runs out, assaulted by the traps he first managed to avoid: blow darts, spikes, pits, closing walls, until he rolls out, covered in cobwebs.

FROM KINESIS TO TENSION

A set piece could begin in kinetic fun, then add tension to create dangerous excitement.

The Incredibles: The film opens with Mr. Incredible rescuing a cat from a tree. This fun then leads Mr. Incredible into an encounter with the villainous French mime Bomb Voyage. Suddenly danger erupts as Bomb Voyage throws an explosive onto a high rail track, blowing a huge gap in the scaffolding, sending a commuter train toward a catastrophic plunge to the street. Mr. Incredible braces himself at the edge of the breach, the train looming closer and closer and closer. This set piece begins in amusing kinesis, then builds tension-filled danger.

IMMEDIATE KINESIS AND TENSION

The first beat of a set piece could electrify instantaneous tension and kinesis. The exhilarating car chases in the *Fast & Furious* franchise start with screeching, smoking tires spinning at the edge of death, followed by smashing windshields and sheering chassis crosscut in rising tension as chaser and pursued wheel toward collision.

The more kinetic yet safe the danger, the more fun the scene. The more dangerous yet still, the more tense. An Action set piece strikes a balance between these poles. To compose one, link the hero to danger.

SET PIECE **MOVEMENTS**

1. HERO MOVES **TOWARD DANGER**
2. HERO MOVES **AWAY FROM DANGER**
3. HERO **FINDS** AND **RESCUES VICTIM**
4. HERO AND VILLAIN **SCRAMBLE FOR MCGUFFIN**
5. HERO **CONFRONTS** VILLAIN

An Action set piece drives a hero in one of five possible directions:

1. The hero moves toward danger.

The hero moves closer and closer to greater and greater jeopardy, often running a gauntlet of threats as he searches, reconnoiters, or attacks.

In *The Lord of the Rings*, Frodo treks through the dangerous lands of Mordor and among monsters along his path.

2. The hero moves away from danger.

To escape, retreat, or maneuver, the hero turns his back on danger.

In the *Bourne* films, chase sequences impel the hero's escape from a corrupt CIA.

3. The hero rescues the victim.

The hero dares danger coming and going as he locates, protects, and rescues the victim.

In *The Dark Knight*, the Joker wedges Batman into a dilemma between rescuing Rachel Dawes, his love, or Harvey Dent, his friend. Batman tries to rescue Rachel only to discover that the Joker has switched the two victims. So, he saves Harvey, the wrong victim, while the Joker kills Rachel.

4. The hero and villain scramble for the MacGuffin.

As hero and villain struggle, the MacGuffin switches from one to the other and back again.

The climax of *Mission: Impossible—Ghost Protocol* pits hero against villain in a high-rise garage. Ethan Hawk and Cobalt scramble for a metallic briefcase containing the key to power over life and death: a device that can disable a nuclear missile.

5. The hero confronts the villain.

The hero comes face-to-face with the villain in a showdown or stalemate. This standoff often turns into a mercy scene, which the hero may or may not survive.

In the finale of *The Perfect Storm*, heroic fishermen at the mercy of the ocean's mountainous swells surrender to their fate.

Like notes on a musical scale, these five movements can be combined, reversed, and composed in an endless variety of ways.

DRAMATIZING SET PIECES

As your hero moves in one of the five possible directions relative to danger within a set piece, what obstacles does he face? What obstructions must he overcome? Within each set piece, the hero's moment-to-moment scrapes and struggles, tactics and exploits call for vivid, specific imaginings.

INTRA-MOVEMENT **CONFLICTS**

1. EXPLORING THE **UNKNOWN**
2. COPING WITH **FRUSTRATIONS / DELAYS**
3. OVERCOMING **LIMITATIONS**
4. REBELLING AGAINST **AUTHORITY**
5. BREAKING **TABOOS**

As noted in Chapter Four, the five techniques that create excitement parallel the five conflicts that add kinesis and tension to set pieces. Once again, they are:

1. Exploring the Unknown

Never-seen-before worlds that contain nameless dangers or mysterious inhabitants put heroes at risk in unforeseeable ways. A hero who can react, adapt, and improvise all-new tactics in an exotic setting fascinates readers and audiences.

2. Overcoming Frustrations and Delays

Cars that won't start, crowd-jammed streets, dead ends, dizzying mazes, empty weapons, and the lies people tell thwart a hero's ingenuity and cool under pressure.

3. Overcoming Limitations

Dark, slippery, shifting, steeply angled terrains that are not just difficult but virtually impossible to navigate test a hero's perseverance and willpower. Settings that force characters together or apart, such as a chasm that must be jumped or a whirlpool that must be escaped, demand all the daring a hero can muster. Limitations within the mind, such as lost memories and unbreakable codes, also add tension and frustration.

4. Rebelling Against Authority

Despotic power invites mutiny. Breaking rules and defying authority add rebellious energy to hero and set piece alike.

The Burj Khalifa sequence in *Mission: Impossible—Ghost Protocol* exploits all four of these techniques: As Ethan Hunt scales the tallest building in the world, he overcomes extreme physical limitations. As he tests equipment he's never used before to master a feat he's never tried before, he explores the unknown. As his magnetic gloves malfunction and the firehose he uses to climb back down comes up short, constant frustrations thwart his perilous climb and force him to jump through an open window three stories below his feet. To climax the sequence, his IMF team breaks into the Burj Khalifa's military-grade computer, rebelling against authority.

5. Breaking Taboos

Unlike the external forces of the four previous techniques, taboos forbid action psychologically and emotionally from within the mind of the hero. Beliefs passed down through cultures, religions, and superstitions erect barricades to the hero's willpower. Like the other four, they too tempt mutiny.

SET PIECES AND CHARACTER

When do we discover the truth about another human being? When do we see below the surface of talk and gesture? In one primal moment: when we witness choice under pressure. How a character chooses to act, instinctively or deliberately, as he pursues desire in the face of conflict reveals his hidden nature. Choices in life-and-death struggles expose the deepest identity. Indeed, the more deadly the conflict, the truer the choice to core self.

So, while the core roles of Action are rarely as psychologically complex as the cast of a character-driven genre, they nonetheless have dimensions needing delineation. In the ideal set piece, characters make choices to take high-risk, death-defying actions that reveal previously unseen qualities. How, for instance, do we know that James Bond is courageous yet cool, fierce yet amused, tenacious yet imaginative?

In the opening series of set pieces in *Casino Royale*, a bomb-carrying killer runs through a massive construction site, a mazelike course of horizontal and vertical obstacles. Bond's courageous choice? To put life at risk and pursue. When the bomber flees with Olympic speed and agility, Bond's choice? Tenacity. He never gives up. When the bomber dives through a vent in a partition, Bond's fierce choice? He rips through the wallboard. When the bomber plays Spider-Man and scampers up scaffolding, Bond's improvisational choice? He commandeers a gigantic crane and topples the structure. Every time the bomber gains a lead, what's Bond's choice? A knowing and amused grin, followed by an improvised solution.

Spider-Man and a scientist-turned-lizard fight for more than ten minutes in *The Amazing Spider-Man*. To propel this sequence, its creators asked themselves, "What would a spider choose?" He would cocoon the monster in a web. "What would a lizard choose?" He would shed his tail to escape capture. "What would a teenager choose?" He would taunt the lizard with trash talk. "What would a scientist choose?" He would concoct a chemical bomb. "What would a hero choose? What would a villain choose?" And so on. The sequence reveals both characterization and core character without exposition, without dialogue, through choices of physical action in a set piece.

Without unique choices, fights become the interchangeable choreography of stock types. Insightful choices that delineate character transform generic scenes into the one-of-a-kind excitement that sustains franchises.

Set Pieces and Turning Points

A set piece that does not change the dynamic charge of Life/Death wastes your talent along with the reader/audience's time and money. Rescue

Scenes change their charge from the edge of death (negative) to beyond the reach of death (positive). Mercy scenes pivot in the opposite direction from freedom (positive) to capture (negative). A flat set piece with no turning point, no change of value charge, cannot be saved by choreography, no matter how kinetic.

Compare two set pieces from *The Matrix* franchise: In *The Matrix*, Neo squares off against Agent Smith. Their kung fu showdown, filled with fantastic stunts, sends them running up the walls of a subway station, dodging bullets, and then wrestling on the tracks as a train screeches toward them.

In the first half of the sequel, *The Matrix Reloaded*, Neo and Smith face off once again, this time in a city park. Neo, now far more powerful than before, contends with an army of Agent Smiths. Dozens upon dozens of Smith clones attack Neo, who retaliates with superheroics, smashing them against lampposts, running over the top of them, even flying.

The five-minute-long subway fight in *The Matrix* engages excitement because the entire set piece hinges around one enormous turning point: To end the fight, Neo does the impossible and defeats Agent Smith. This negative to positive turn leads Neo to believe that he is The One.

The ten-minute brawl in *The Matrix Reloaded*, one martial arts stunt after another, goes nowhere. This flat set piece bores almost immediately. It merely delivers exposition: Agent Smith is back and there are lots of him.

The Kinetic Setting

Open spaces tend to limit action. Enemies facing each other across a battlefield or rolling sea shrinks the expanse to heighten suspense but offers few surprises. The same is true in imagination-starved settings with dented cars exploding into fireballs or flaying bodies falling slo-mo from high-rises—stunts we have seen again and again. To fulfill your personal vision, create a setting that's kinetically alive with never-seen-before people and powers, objects and barriers, realities and temporalities that demand ingenious writing.

Three examples:

Die Hard explores an executive high-rise, still under construction. From basement to rooftop, floor after floor offers opportunities for creative action. The heliport, for instance, conceals a bomb, while upper stories weave a maze of vents and open shafts, support beams and loose wiring, whirring fans and power tools, debris strewn everywhere—all waiting to become a weapon or a trap.

In *The Wrath of Khan*, Captains Kirk and Khan search for each other inside a nebula so thick with radioactive haze that their ships' sensors read nothing but static. This setting blinds both hero and villain, forcing them to rely on reason and imagination.

In *Police Story 4: First Strike*, Jackie Chan fights dozens of adversaries in a banquet hall, yet he manages to transform this space into a cornucopia of weapons. When set upon, Chan dives behind a table, flips it over, and propels it across the floor, scattering his aggressors. He uses their clothing as weapons, tying them up in their jackets and ties. Finally, he choreographs an extended fight up, in, and around a stepladder.

A Note on Kinetic Choreography

If you write Action novels, kinesis must spiral out of your word pictures. The images you paint with language, whether literal or metaphorical, must stimulate the mind's eye of the reader with vivid, pulsating energy. No small task. Read, for example, the powerfully kinetic prose imagery in the novel *The North Water*.

If you create graphic novels, an illustrator, you or a collaborator, must render kinetic action in motionless images. Again, no small task.

If you write for the screen, whether a fiction acted by actors or a game played by a player, your set pieces will be choreographed by other people. Teams that create production designs, stunts, and sound effects will stage, shoot, or animate images that editors and composers ultimately cut and score. Elaborate verbal descriptions of blow-by-blow action on pages of a screenplay annoy these people. Only give them what they need, and "They fight" is often enough.

13

PRAISE AND MOCKERY

Set pieces modulate intensity visually and physically, but sounds and words also propel events. As the saying goes, "*Words kill.*" Dialogue to add wit and irony while increasing tension is one of Action's many delights. (See *Dialogue: The Art of Verbal Action for Page, Stage, and Screen.*)

For the Action writer, praise and mockery offer two sharp-edged tactics. In most cases, critical or complimentary dialogue is direct and to the point. But in some cases, acclaim takes the form of a complaint: "She's as stealthful as a shark," for instance, is ironic praise.

Any dialogue that mocks the power of a hero or villain diminishes them; any words that praise their power heighten them—in the mind of the audience/reader. And this is the point of dialogue that celebrates or vilifies: It shapes the storygoer's image of these characters and her feelings toward them. Below are a few select examples.

THE SPEECH IN PRAISE OF THE VILLAIN

Powerful people get talked about. In Action, the villain weighs on everyone's mind, so the cast naturally talks about her mentality, powers, and plans. This dialogue often takes the form of a warning that implicitly praises the villain and thus enhances her overdog stature.

In *Alien*, Ripley asks Ash, a robot, for advice on how to kill the alien.

ASH: *(with a sly smile)* You still don't understand what you're dealing with, do you? A perfect organism. Its structural

> perfection is matched only by its hostility. I admire its purity. A survivor. Unclouded by conscience, remorse, or delusions of morality. I can't lie to you about your chances, but you have my sympathies.

Speeches in praise of the villain not only increase her presence but give the writer the means to dramatize exposition and pass it easily to the audience/reader.

In *The Dark Knight*, Batman dismisses the Joker as just another criminal, but Alfred warns him:

> **ALFRED:** Some men aren't looking for anything logical. They can't be bought, bullied, reasoned with, or negotiated with. Some men just want to watch the world burn.

In *No Country for Old Men*, Llewelyn Moss finds a briefcase full of drug money in the desert and runs off. The cartel hires a psychopath, Anton Chigurh, to get it back. After a shootout between Moss and Chigurh, the wounded Moss escapes to Mexico and seeks treatment in a hospital. Carson Wells, a second hired gun, tracks him there and tries to make a deal for the missing cash, but Moss resists.

> **LLEWELYN MOSS:** If I was cutting deals, why wouldn't I go deal with this guy Chigurh?
>
> **CARSON WELLS:** No, no, no, you don't understand. You can't make a deal with him. Even if you gave him the money, he'd still kill you. He's a peculiar man. You could even say he has principles. Principles that transcend money or drugs or anything like that. He's not like you. He's not even like me.

With these warnings, writers intensify their villain's dark powers, portraying them as essentially inhuman predators, building their overdog status in the imagination of the audience/reader.

The Action villain loves her scheme, her perfect crime. But her triumph can only be sweet if she can parade her genius and righteousness before the hero. Vanity and narcissism bring out her braggadocio, so with that in mind, some writers give the speech in praise of the villain to the villain.

In *The Dark Knight*, Batman confronts the Joker:

BATMAN: Why do you want to kill me?
JOKER: I don't want to kill you. What would I do without you? Go back to ripping off mob dealers? No. No. No. No, you complete me... I'm not a monster. I'm just ahead of the curve. The only sensible way to live in this world is without rules. Nothing can threaten me.

As the real-life villain, the Marquis de Sade, once bragged: "Through cruelty one rises to heights of superhuman sensitivity and awareness that cannot be reached any other way."

With a well-executed turning point, praise for a supporting character can ironically transfer to the villain. In *Guardians of the Galaxy*, convicts in the most dangerous prison in the galaxy speak in terrified wonder of the magnificently muscled Drax the Destroyer. But when Drax faces Ronan the Accuser, the villain who killed Drax's own family, Ronan thrashes Drax and drowns him in a vat of chemicals. Suddenly, the awe and praise for Drax transfers to Ronan.

THE SPEECH IN PRAISE OF THE HERO

High acclaim for the protagonist risks turning an underdog into an overdog. For that reason, dialogue praising a story's hero is rare. Praise, however, when said with simple, calm confidence, can enhance a hero's aura without undoing the disparity in power between villain and hero.

In *Taken*, as Bryan Mills talks to his daughter on the phone, he hears slave traders break into her hotel room and kidnap her. When a man named Marko picks up the phone, Mills says:

BRYAN MILLS: I don't know who you are. I don't know what you want. If you're looking for ransom, I can tell you I don't have any money. But what I do have is a very particular set of skills. Skills that I have acquired over a long career. Skills that make me a nightmare for people like you. If you let my daughter go now, that will be the end of it. I will not look for you, I will not pursue you. But if you don't, I will look for you. I will find you. I will kill you.

THE SPEECH IN MOCKERY OF THE HERO

Sharp-worded, well-timed mockery helps keep a hero, even one with the prestige of James Bond, an underdog. In the Bond series, M serves that purpose. Cold and blunt, she initially dislikes Bond, whom she calls:

> **M:** . . . a sexist, misogynist dinosaur, a relic of the Cold War whose boyish charms, though wasted on me, only appeal to young girls.

When Raoul Silva, *Skyfall's* villain, first appears, his men have strapped Bond to a chair.

> **SILVA:** Just look at you, barely held together by pills and drink. Did M tell you the psychologist cleared you for duty?
>
> **BOND:** Yes.

Silva accesses Bond's evaluation results from a computer and reads them aloud:

> **SILVA:** "Medical evaluation: fail. Physical evaluation: fail. Psychological evaluation: alcohol and substance addiction indicated."*(in mock shock)* Oof! *(back to reading)* "Pathological rejection of authority based on unresolved childhood trauma. Subject is not approved for field duty and immediate suspension from service advised." *(grinning at Bond)* M sent you after me, knowing you're not ready, knowing you would likely die. Mommy was very bad.

The most relentless lampooning of the hero punctuates Action Comedies. Ensemble teams of heroes in satires such as *Men in Black*, *Galaxy Quest*, and *Guardians of the Galaxy* taunt one another mercilessly.

Speeches deriding the hero help swing the balance of power toward the villain, but as effective as they may be, words cannot substitute for deeds. This is especially true of mockery aimed at the villain.

THE SPEECH IN MOCKERY OF THE VILLAIN

Mockery of the villain may demonstrate the hero's wit under pressure, but too much sarcasm, too often said, can reverse the underdog/overdog imbalance of power and sour excitement.

The team of heroes in *The Avengers*, for instance, relentlessly mock the villainous Norse god Loki. Bruce Banner says Loki's as mad as a bag of cats, while Nick Fury compares him to an insect. Tony Stark mocks Loki four times in one scene alone: He sneers at Loki's plan and calls his magic scepter a "glowstick." Loki brags that he has an army, but Tony Stark laughs it off: "We have a Hulk." Indeed, at story climax, the Hulk mocks Loki's puny powers and throws him around like a rag doll. Finally, when the god tries to manipulate Iron Man's mind and fails, Tony Stark likens Loki's flaccid telepathy to sexual impotence.

One or two such moments might have been amusing, but taken together, continuous insults by the entire cast of heroes created a tide of mockery that washed away Loki's aura of power and dampened the thrills in an otherwise highly successful film.

When well used, however, mockery of the villain often becomes an excellent ploy to set up a key turning point.

In a season finale of *Doctor Who*, the Doctor travels back in time to Stonehenge in AD 200. Underneath the world-famous stone circle, a gigantic technological box called the Pandorica lies hidden. Inside waits the most fearsome being in the universe. The Doctor finds the Pandorica, but just as it starts to open, alien spaceships appear in the night sky over Stonehenge.

Over the five decades of this series, the Doctor has defeated every alien menace he's ever faced. It seems a bit ridiculous that they still bother to scheme against him. And yet multiple, varied alien ships now zoom in circles above Stonehenge, ready to open the Pandorica and seize the galactic terror lurking inside. The Doctor looks up:

<u>THE DOCTOR:</u> Who takes the Pandorica, takes the universe, but, bad news everyone, 'cause guess who...? *(annoyed by the busy ships)* Ha! Listen, you lot, you're all whizzing about. It's very distracting. Could you all just stay still for a minute because I. AM. TALKING.

The spaceships stop, stationary in the sky.

<u>THE DOCTOR:</u> *(cont'd)* Now the question of the hour is: "Who's got the Pandorica?" Answer: I do. Next question: "Who's coming to take it from me?"

None of the spaceships move.

<u>THE DOCTOR:</u> *(cont'd)* Come ooonnn! Look at me! As you're sitting up there in your silly little spaceships with all your silly little guns, just remember who's standing in your way. Remember every black day I ever stopped you. And then, AND THEN, do the smart thing: Let somebody else go first.

One by one, the ships think about it and then flee.

In the underground structure, however, the Pandorica continues to hum, slowly opening itself. The Doctor gazes inside and... nothing. Empty.

Suddenly, dozens of Doctor Who's nemeses reappear. Working together for the first time, the aliens grab the Doctor and lock him inside the Pandorica, the perfect prison they designed to hold him for eternity. Now the box does indeed house the most fearsome being in the universe: the Doctor. By indulging in mockery, the hero traps himself in the mercy scene.

14
CRISIS AND CLIMAX

THE ACTION ARC

Arcs trace change: either a beginning-to-end change in the charge of a story's core value or a transformation within a character's inner self.

Arcs in the Action Genre are almost always of the first kind. They change the outer fortunes of a cast, most often moving the story's core value from death to life for hero and victim and from life to death for the villain. Over the course of change, characters reveal their inner natures, but their essential selves stay unchanged from beginning through to the end.

If a writer wishes to arc his hero's deep character, he must merge the Action Plot with one of the six genres of inner change, such as the Redemption Plot (a bad guy turns good) or the Degeneration Plot (the good guy turns bad). (See *Character: The Art of Role and Cast Design for Page, Stage, and Screen.*)

CRISIS: THE HERO'S ULTIMATE CHOICE

Throughout the hero's story-long spine of action he strives to save the victim, improvising one strategy after another, each more arduous and dangerous than the one before, until he confronts the final clash. Face-to-face with the most powerful, sharply focused weapon in the villain's arsenal, he must choose his final action. This is the *crisis*: All points of no return passed, all possible tactics tried and failed... save one.

This scene raises the final question in the reader/audience: Just how heroic is the hero? The answer, acted out under maximum pressure, demands the Action writer's most creative insights.

How a hero chooses to act in this moment expresses his breadth of courage, his range of skills, his cool under pressure, and, most important, his commitment to altruism. The Action crisis puts the hero's code to the test: Will he sacrifice his life for the life of another?

In most Action Stories, the crisis decision tightens suspense in the very last sequence and then triggers the last-act climax. In *Guardians of the Galaxy*, for example, Quill, Drax, Rocket, Groot, and Gamora join forces in the final confrontation, risking and even sacrificing their lives for one another and for the millions on Xandar.

In some works, however, the hero makes his crisis decision almost immediately. Rather than a choice to end the spine of action, in stories starring characters like Ethan Hunt and James Bond, the hero's key decision turns the inciting incident and starts the spine of action. The telling then builds cycles of rising conflict over the acts that follow, until the risks and tensions pay off in the culminating climax.

In Bond films, M calls James into her office and tells him about a master criminal out to destroy civilization as we know it today. M says it's up to Bond to stop him. Bond nods and says, "All right, I'll do it." With that, he pursues his story-long quest for the villain, never making another crisis decision.

Mission: Impossible—Ghost Protocol begins with four individual crisis decisions. In Act One, IMF's control offers Ethan Hunt a mission that, should he accept it, will sever him from the US government and brand him a fugitive. He, of course, accepts. Later, Ethan makes the same offer to his three fellow agents. Carter accepts without hesitation; Benji resignedly admits that their mission must be taken. Brandt, on the other hand, needs a compelling reason to sacrifice his life. He resists until he realizes that the only way to prevent nuclear holocaust is to back Ethan's play.

THE ACTION CLIMAX

Whether the crisis decision is toward the beginning or near the end, it sets up the ultimate ending. Most Action Stories climax fully positive: villain defeated, lives saved. A few fully negative: villain victorious, lives lost. Yet others end in one of two ironies: villain defeated and lives saved but the hero is dead; or villain triumphant and lives lost but the survivors discover an important truth.

The vast majority of Action Stories climax on an up-ending for this reason: The storyteller promises a positive experience; therefore, he must keep his promise.

At the inciting incident of most Action tales, villains wield phenomenal life-and-death power. From that point on, conflict foregrounds excitement but keeps dread out of sight. This flow of pleasureful thrills foreshadows a climax in which a courageous underdog will turn tables on a heinous overdog. The wide-eyed fun that this design augurs must not be spoiled.

Should the storytelling do the opposite—should it foreground dread and diminish excitement—then the writer promises an overall negative ending. And again, promises must be kept, as in *Avengers: Infinity War*, *Batman V Superman*, and *No Time to Die*.

Tragic Action tales thrill us for a very different reason. When the dark side of human nature defeats a noble soul or a righteous cause, the reader/audience discovers a hidden truth, an assertion of realistic probability over unrealistic hope. Even though dark endings express truthful psychological and sociological insights, Action Stories such as *The Grey*, *Logan*, and *No Country for Old Men* are the exception.

Finally, if the end effect is an absolute positive, then the villain's defeat must also be absolute. This is especially the case for villains whose menace comes chiefly from their mystery. Secrets shroud the T-1000 in *Terminator 2* and Aldrich Killian in *Iron Man 3*. No one knows the range and variety of their powers. Before they die, they must be fully exposed, nothing left hidden. Otherwise, the reader/audience suspects that the villain has something up his sleeve and could come back to life from a seeming death.

DEFEAT OF THE VILLAIN

With the balance of power tilted powerfully toward a villain who's immune to the hero's tactics, how can the hero defeat this character finally and absolutely?

Like the mercy scene tactics from Chapter Four, here are the four that can shape an Action climax:

1. Overwhelm him.

A hero can overpower a villain in one of two ways. First, he can master the villain's weapon. In *Batman Begins*, Bruce Wayne overpowers Ra's al Ghul using the combat techniques his teacher taught him. Or second, the hero can fulfill his potential. In *The Matrix*, Neo's innate but unrealized willpower eventually conquers Agent Smith.

2. Outsmart him.

As the hero's every attempt fails, he keeps striving to discover a new weapon or tactic until he eventually finds a weakness in the villain, a way to puncture his immunity.

In *Star Trek: The Wrath of Khan*, Kirk first uses a prefix code, which buys time, but Khan won't fall for that trick a second time. So, Kirk tries to bait Khan, but Khan remains cautious. Eventually, Kirk outsmarts and defeats Khan when he discovers Khan's weakness: Khan does not think in the three dimensions of outer-space combat, but in two dimensions as if their fight were grounded on a planet.

3. Outnumber him.

Some heroes gather an arsenal of weapons (*Iron Man*) or an ensemble of sidekicks (*X-Men*). In either case, they end up having to combine, with ingenuity, these disparate powers and abilities to defeat the villain. In a delightfully toyetic concept, the cast of *Voltron* literally combines.

4. Leverage the MacGuffin.

Sometimes the MacGuffin itself can be used as a weapon against the villain, as in *Galaxy Quest*. Throughout the film, the evil alien Sarris seeks the Omega 13 device. No one knows for sure what it can do, but the prevailing theory suggests it resets time by thirteen seconds—time enough to fix a single mistake. At the climax, Sarris storms the bridge of the *Protector*, killing the crew. Nesmith manages to activate the Omega 13 and with his thirteen seconds, turns the tables on Sarris and revives the crew.

These four means can be mixed and merged in endless recombinations.

THE FALSE ENDING

Some stories climax, but then, in the last moments, the villain comes back to life. Known in Hollywood as *killing 'em dead*, the villain's resurrection delivers a final thrill before he's unequivocally executed.

In *Die Hard*, after Hans Gruber falls to his death, Karl, his lieutenant, suddenly reappears, only to be shot dead by Powell, the hero's sidekick. The villain-rising-from-the-dead device is yet another magnet for clichés.

THE RESOLUTION SCENE

An Action climax immediately impacts its three core characters, but the audience may be curious about its rippling effect in the greater world. A resolution scene may be needed, therefore, to show how the ending spreads throughout the story's setting. In the final scenes of *Avatar*, for example, nearly all the humans on the planet Pandora are expelled. A glorious Pandoran victory celebration ends the film.

In some rare tellings, an unfinished subplot could extend past the central plot's climax. This subplot will need a separate ending to close the work. This, however, often feels awkward and anticlimactic. The central plot is the story's emotional heart, and the telling should end when it ends.

15

PACE AND PROGRESSION

Like a Broadway musical, an Action Story ebbs and surges with pulsing cycles of rising tension. Like song-and-dance numbers, set pieces burst with explosive kinesis, each singing a new tune. Progressive Action opens with an inciting incident that compels involvement, orchestrates the pace of its complications to build high excitement, and climaxes on a crescendo of elation.

To achieve this compelling effect, the Action author evolves her story along three dimensions: rhythm, tempo, intensity. Lengths of scenes govern storytelling rhythm; the energy within a scene sets its tempo; proximity to danger charges a scene's intensity. An Action writer conducts a story by harmonizing these three qualities into scenes, sequences, and set pieces that forge ahead—never repeating, never digressing, always building excitement to climax.

SET PIECE RHYTHM

The length, spacing, and pacing of scenes toe-tap a story's rhythm. It may be tempting to pit your hero against your villain in one standoff after another, but back-to-back-to-back confrontations actually drain interest. The drumbeat of repetition kills excitement.

Interest deepens, on the other hand, as scenes of varying content get shorter and shorter, accelerating pace in an ever-tightening sequence. When this brisk rhythm peaks, it earns a pause. Here the writer hits the brakes and focuses the audience on a major set piece, a powerful turning point that takes all the time it needs.

PRINCIPLE: Progression, not repetition.

Rising cycles of ever-quickening scenes, capped off by major set pieces, build an impactful Action Story. So, to shape your progressions, list the major turning points in your story's step-outline, then rank them by impact. If your story calls for six set pieces, for example, number the least impactful as #1, the most impactful as #6, and the other four in between by order of impact.

Contrary to instinct, however, performing set pieces in a 1-2-3-4-5-6 pattern is not the most effective progression because a weak start doesn't grab interest. Instead, open strong with one of your major actions, then build to the most powerful. A 4-1-2-3-5-6 order hooks involvement, backs off a bit, then progresses with intensity and excitement to climax.

VARIETY

Repetition creates a three-part pattern:

The first use of a technique generates its full effect; the second use delivers half or less than half of the previous effect; the third use reverses itself and causes the opposite, progression killing effect.

Set pieces, therefore, no matter how kinetic or intense, cannot repeat the same movement (attack, attack, attack). Repetition not only slows the story's progression, but breeds anti-excitement and sends the telling into retreat. To inspire progressive variety, explore all five Action set pieces and vary their inner movements.

There is, however, this exception: The same movement can be recycled if the cast creates variety. In *The Avengers*, confrontations repeat with entertaining differences as Captain America fights Loki, Thor battles Iron Man, Captain America teams up with Iron Man against the Chitauri, Thor takes on the Hulk, the Hulk attacks Loki, and on it goes.

CROSSCUTTING

Every set piece has a natural rise and fall. Crosscutting between two or more parallel set pieces eliminates unnecessary ebbs and concentrates on critical flows. By cutting away before energy fades, excitement progresses higher and higher, peak to peak.

Finding Nemo crosscuts between two simultaneous set pieces: Marlin's hunt for his son Nemo moves toward danger, while Nemo's struggle to escape a dental office aquarium moves away from danger. When the suspense-filled jeopardy of Marlin's transoceanic adventures tops out, the telling cuts to Nemo's predicament. As that conflict turns, a crosscut takes us back to Marlin's struggle, then back to Nemo again, thus focusing on intense actions while keeping the audience in high suspense.

PACING IMPACT

Cutting from peak to peak to peak, however, risks repetition. An Action story line, therefore, needs to shift gears now and then—take another point of view, strike a contrasting tone, or open a subplot in different genre.

The Incredibles, for instance, weaves two genres: an Action central plot intercut with a Social Drama subplot. Scenes in which the family of superheroes copes with social prejudices against them space out the Action set pieces. As a result, the battles of Incredibles versus Syndrome feel progressive, not redundant.

Guardians of the Galaxy counterpoints drama with comedy to give the telling playful tonal variations. The prison breakout set piece, for instance, starts in high tension as Peter Quill and his fellow heroes escape a den of murderous inmates and guards. But then the drama pivots to comedy when Peter runs back inside to rescue a cassette player that holds his favorite tunes.

PACING VALUE CHARGES

Repetition annoys us, but it reaches its most irritating state when the same value charge echoes in scene after scene—either positive, positive, positive or negative, negative, negative. To hold interest, alternate value charges between turning points and within scenes: Start a scene on a positive note, then swing to the negative, or do the reverse. Then alternate the charges at the ends of scenes. If dynamic change becomes too rapid, however, it may appear capricious and random. If it's too subtle, it may feel repetitive.

To further avoid repetition and generate variety, turn events on contrasting values. In *Ghost Protocol*, Justice/Injustice comes into play when the Russian police close in on Ethan Hunt. Life/Death enters the telling as the IMF team faces one high-risk set piece after another. Finally, the villain pushes War/Peace closer and closer to nuclear holocaust.

You can, of course, alternate charges from beat to beat within a scene. Consider this from *Iron Man 3*:

While chatting in a small-town bar, Tony Stark gets a lead on the villain (good news), but he's suddenly handcuffed by a woman impersonating a Homeland Security agent (bad news). When the local sheriff demands her ID (good news), she kills him using superpowers (bad news). Stark escapes (good news), but she finds him (bad news). Stark tries to strangle her with the handcuffs (good news), but she melts the steel (bad news). Stark creates a wall of fire to keep her at bay (good news), but she walks through the fire (bad news), and into Stark's trap, a massive gas explosion that destroys her (best news).

MODULATING TEMPO

The greater the energy, the greater the excitement. Too much fluctuation, however, wears an audience out, constant oscillation taxing their concentration, causing them to lose track and lose interest. But if kinetic energy remains too low, the audience changes channels. The skill of the writer, as always, balances the extremes of "too little" and "too much."

To win the war against repetitious action, consider these five strategies for modulating tempo:

1. Accelerate activity.

The simplest tactic quickens choreography by constantly accelerating pace as cars speed past and shots fly. This transcends media. The novelist, for example, uses words to create high-paced images: Bullets whiz past heads, motorcycles race through twisting turns, people leap across rooftops. All of this can be counterpointed with slow drifting, dragging, floating language, so that when the speed picks up pace again, it invigorates even more energy.

The novel can excite kinetics by the way the author describes set pieces, but film offers thrice the tools because the screen has three orders of movement: the actions of the characters within their setting, the actions of the camera filming them, and the editing of those images. The screenwriter can contrast slow movements with fast, but also call on a traveling camera, shifting angles, and counterpointing editing.

To exploit the dynamic between static versus swift movements, *The Matrix*'s filmmakers created Bullet Time to dramatize Neo's bullet-dodging skills. They first use a fixed camera when Neo fights with lightning-fast flurries of punches and kicks. But when he's shot at, the film slows to an ultra-slow, near-freeze-frame pace, allowing Neo to move out of the path of oncoming bullets. Then while Neo and the bullets hang in the air, the camera quick-pans with whirlwind speed.

2. Merge set pieces.

When set pieces combine, energy builds. A set piece that merges an escape with a rescue fuses two movements into one, doubling risk and jeopardy. If those two set pieces combine with a fight for the MacGuffin, kinetics redoubles.

In the climax of *The Dark Knight*, Batman tracks the Joker to the top of a skyscraper covered with scaffolding. Below on the Gotham River float two ferryboats: one filled with civilians, the other with prison inmates. Both are at the Joker's mercy because he has hidden a bomb in each ferry but put the detonators in opposite boats. The Joker's game? One group must blow up the other or he will destroy both at once.

What's more, on the upper reaches of the scaffolding, the Joker's henchmen stand guard over hostages. Batman goes in ahead of the SWAT team only to discover the depths of the Joker's ingenuity: He has disguised the hostages as kidnappers and dressed the kidnappers as hostages. The Joker wants the SWAT team to kill the hostages, so his henchmen can kill the SWAT team. Batman will have to rescue not only the hostages but the SWAT team, too. And he must somehow rescue the people on the two ferryboats. In this climactic set piece, Batman confronts danger, moves into danger, and pulls off three rescues. Each choice and action Batman makes and takes resonates across five lines of action.

3. Accelerate rhythm.

Beyond kinetics of tempo inside scenes, the pace of turning points also stimulates excitement: The closer and closer come reversals, the faster and faster climaxes pile up, the more intense the telling.

In the last two acts in *Mission: Impossible—Ghost Protocol*, the film quickens pace across many major turning points. In one of them, for instance, the IMF team sends Brandt into a computer system guarded by a gigantic whirling fan, only to have Cobalt take control of the system, overheat the fan, and spin it out of control. Brandt's escape from this searing death trap turns the film's tenth set piece.

The IMF team then tracks Cobalt to Mumbai and the eleventh set piece sends Ethan and Carter rushing through jammed traffic to capture Cobalt, but before they can reach him, he tricks a Russian submarine into firing a nuclear missile at San Francisco.

Seconds count down as Ethan's dogged pursuit of Cobalt crosscuts with his team's shoot-out with Cobalt's henchman. Ethan finally corners the villain in a scramble for the device that arms the missile. As his team kills the henchman, Ethan kills Cobalt and takes control of the MacGuffin. He disarms the missile a split second before it lands. These climactic turning points—moving into danger, escape from danger, chase, shoot-out, scramble—interlink five set pieces in seven minutes.

The entire film, of course, could not run at that pounding pace. Instead, it starts fast, then slows before getting faster yet, pausing again before accelerating, building in cycles before holding nothing back for the last act's climax.

4. Contrast settings.

Varying the setting offers an expensive yet eye-pleasing way to create variety. Traveling franchises like the Bond films vary exotic, opulent locations one after another. In *Mission: Impossible—Ghost Protocol*, the many movements away from and toward danger globe-trot from the Russian Kremlin to the Burj Khalifa to an automated vertical carpark in Mumbai, breathing excitement into what could have been repetitive stunts.

5. Crosscut for kinesis.

Crosscutting offers yet another means to increase kinesis. A telling could cut between the points of view of various characters, between locations in space, between locations in time (past, present, future), or between plot and subplot.

Rockstar Games' *Grand Theft Auto V* crosscuts the story lines of three hero-villains: ex-bank-robber Michael De Santa, gangster Franklin Clinton, and drug dealer–gunrunner Trevor Philips.

MODULATING INTENSITY

As odds against survival rise higher and higher, excitement intensifies. As with all other facets of Action writing, thrills must be shaped and paced. The following five techniques modulate intensity within the strategies listed above.

1. Close distance to danger.

Whether escaping a death trap or running a gauntlet of foes, the closer and closer the hero comes to death, the more and more intense the excitement. The term *cliffhanger*, for instance, originated in mid-twentieth-century Saturday afternoon movie serials. An Action hero would end an episode dangling from a cliff, the story waiting to be resolved in next week's episode. Cliffhanging arouses a week's worth of excitement by telescoping the closeness of death down to fingertips clinging to a rock.

The rescue set piece from *Terminator 2* progressively shortens the distance to death in eleven steps:

1. Young John Connor wants to rescue his mother from an insane asylum. His guardian Terminator argues against the idea, knowing the T-1000 will be waiting for them. As they debate this move, they're miles away from death.
2. John and the Terminator invade the asylum to break out Sarah Connor.
3. But the T-1000 suddenly appears, standing behind a security gate. The villain nonchalantly melts his way through the bars.

4. But his gun gets caught in the barrier. He is now about fifty feet away from the escaping trio.
5. John and his mother run to an elevator. The Terminator fires shotgun rounds at the T-1000, buying time for the trio to dodge inside the elevator as the doors close—the villain is now two or three steps away.
6. The T-1000 jumps down the shaft and onto the roof of the elevator. His forearms morph into huge knives, blindly stabbing through the ceiling as the elevator doors open in a parking garage. The T-1000 can almost grab them.
7. Rushing out of the elevator, Sarah commandeers a police car. The T-800 drives as Sarah rides shotgun with John in the back seat. Now a few yards separate them from the T-1000.
8. The T-1000 pours through holes in the elevator roof, retakes its human form, and sprints after the car. The Terminator, without enough time to turn the car around, reverses out of the garage. Once outside, he grabs the hand brake and spins the car around, speeding off.
9. The turning action, however, gives the T-1000 time to catch up. His hands form into hooks as he latches onto the car's rear bumper, now just feet away.
10. The Terminator wheels around corners at high speed, scraping the T-1000 against the asphalt, but it pulls itself up onto the car, smashing through the rear window, lashing out at John, just inches away.
11. Sarah takes the wheel so the Terminator can lean out the window. His shotgun blasts loosen the T-1000's hooks from the car, sending the villain clanging and clattering across the road. The trio of heroes speed away, putting miles between them and the villain.

Our pulse quickens as this set piece modulates the proximity to danger, drawing the T-1000 closer and closer to John Connor, the film's MacGuffin.

2. Multiply values.

The core value of Life/Death drives all Action Stories. In *Terminator 2*, for instance, all conflict pivots that sole value and none other. But in many tellings, Life/Death compounds with other values to heighten excitement.

In *The Fugitive*, every scene in which Kimble eludes Deputy Gerard turns the value of not only Life/Death, but also Justice/Injustice as he struggles to apprehend the man who murdered his wife.

Guardians of the Galaxy weaves a complex of four values: The heroes risk Freedom versus Prison when they ask Nova Corps for help. On the personal level, they wrestle back and forth between Friendship and Enmity, while on an even deeper level, their consciences war with Morality (risking their lives to save others) versus Immorality (selfishly trying to save themselves). Overall, of course, the core value of Life/Death governs the film. All four values twist and turn until the climax delivers a positive charge for each.

3. Progress the stakes.

Stories can progress widely into society and the physical world or deeply into their characters' minds and emotions. In some cases, both. By progressing what the characters risk and how far they are willing to go to get what they want, danger increases as they give up more of their personal safety and inner security to save more of the world and the lives within it.

Compare *The Avengers* with *Guardians of the Galaxy*. In *The Avengers*, risk remains static. From start to finish, the Avengers risk their lives but nothing outside of that or within themselves. When *Guardians of the Galaxy* begins, Star-Lord refuses to even risk a paycheck, but at the climax, he puts his life on the line, plus the lives of his friends, plus their self-respect as heroes, plus twelve billion souls on Xandar. The more is at risk, the greater the intensity of excitement.

4. Deepen and widen villainy.

The five story lines in the *Bourne* series peel away layer upon layer of villainy hidden within a maze of government bureaucracy.

In *The Dark Knight*, the Joker treasures the evil within himself, but takes the greatest delight in exposing the evil lurking within heroes such as Harvey Dent and Batman himself.

5. Polarize risk.

Total success and absolute failure bracket a spectrum of human effort that runs in degrees from one end to the other. But when intensity reaches its maximum, the middle ground vanishes and risk becomes all-or-nothing, win-or-lose, no wiggle room.

In *Star Wars*, Luke Skywalker has no second chance—just one shot at the Death Star.

As a hero's options become fewer and fewer, jeopardy concentrates, and risk becomes greater and greater even though the stakes remain the same.

In *Mission: Impossible—Ghost Protocol*, the IMF team members risk their lives as soon as they accept their mission, but they only have one chance to intercept the codes, one chance to stop the launch, one chance to abort the warhead. They don't even have time to plan. Each failure forces the IMF to greater desperation in their attempts to stop Cobalt. Races against time, such as those in *Ghost Protocol*, polarize risk by reducing the resources at the heroes' disposal and the opportunity to recover from failure. Peril becomes certain and imminent. The closer their choice comes to all-or-nothing, the more intense the danger.

CASE STUDY: *DIE HARD*

Die Hard orchestrates rhythm, tempo, and intensity, employing all five varieties of Action movement over eight set pieces. Let's survey this classic, starting with a review of the film's eight set pieces, and then a look at how the expressive techniques explored in this chapter harmonize within the telling.

The Eight Set Pieces of *Die Hard*

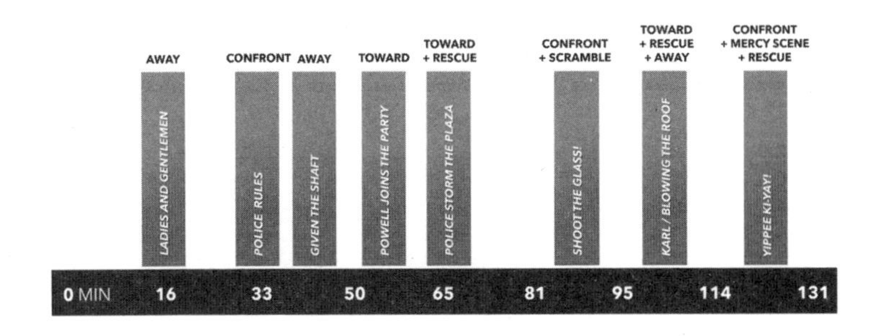

1. Escaping Danger

DIE HARD: SET PIECE 1

MOVEMENT: **AWAY**

Fifteen minutes into the film, Hans Gruber and his crew of fake terrorists invade Nakatomi Plaza, killing anyone in their way, taking a roomful of terrified hostages. John McClane—shirtless, barefoot, gun in hand—escapes unnoticed.

---

2. Confronting Danger

DIE HARD: SET PIECE 2

MOVEMENT: **CONFRONT**

Later, McClane tries to arrest Gruber's right-hand goon Karl, but, unfazed, Karl tries to kill McClane.

3. Escaping Danger

DIE HARD: SET PIECE 3

McClane cuts and runs into an air vent.

4. Moving into Danger

DIE HARD: SET PIECE 4

Police officer Powell checks out Nakatomi Plaza and determines that nothing is wrong. As he goes back in his patrol car, McClane kills a Gruber henchman, throwing the body out a window, crashing into Powell's patrol car, forcing the cops to act.

5. *Into Danger / Rescuing Victim*

DIE HARD: SET PIECE 5

A SWAT team storms the plaza, but Gruber's minions fire military-grade weaponry onto the unsuspecting, outgunned, ill-prepared LAPD. McClane once again moves into danger as he takes on the terrorists, giving cover and rescuing the fleeing SWAT team.

6. *Scramble for MacGuffin*

Gruber's scheme calls for an enormous explosion on the roof that will kill the hostages, fake his own death, and cover his escape, but for that he needs a stash of detonators—*Die Hard*'s MacGuffin. At first McClane runs for the MacGuffin, but Gruber wins the scramble by covering the floor surrounding the detonators with shards of broken glass, so that the barefoot McClane can't get back to them in time.

DIE HARD: SET PIECE 6

MOVEMENT: **CONFRONT + SCRAMBLE**

7. Rushing into Danger / Rescuing Victims / Escaping Danger

DIE HARD: SET PIECE 7

MOVEMENT: **TOWARD + RESCUE + AWAY**

In a three-movement penultimate set piece, McClane races to the roof for a showdown with Karl. He kills Karl and rescues the hostages just before Gruber's bombs detonate. McClane then ties himself to a fire hose and dives off the exploding roof. Dangling thirty floors up, he kicks through a window and crashes inside, the fire hose almost dragging him to his death.

8. Mercy Scene / Confronting Danger / Rescuing Victim

DIE HARD: SET PIECE 8

The final three-movement set piece begins with a mercy scene in which McClane outwits the villain with a gun duct-taped to his bare back, followed by a final confrontation with Gruber and the rescue of his wife as together they watch Gruber plunge to his death.

Set Piece Progression

The high impact of *Die Hard*'s opening set piece hooks the audience into the telling. The second set piece then lowers intensity while setting the stage so that the next six can top one another, each surpassing the one that came before.

Set Piece Length

Powerful events need screen time. If a set piece goes by quickly, its impact seems slight no matter the cost of lives. A sudden, unexpected explosion that kills millions may surprise the audience but still feel minor because the experience lasts only a second or two.

If a set piece spins into action immediately on the heels of the previous set piece, it seems repetitious and impact shrivels. A space of time between

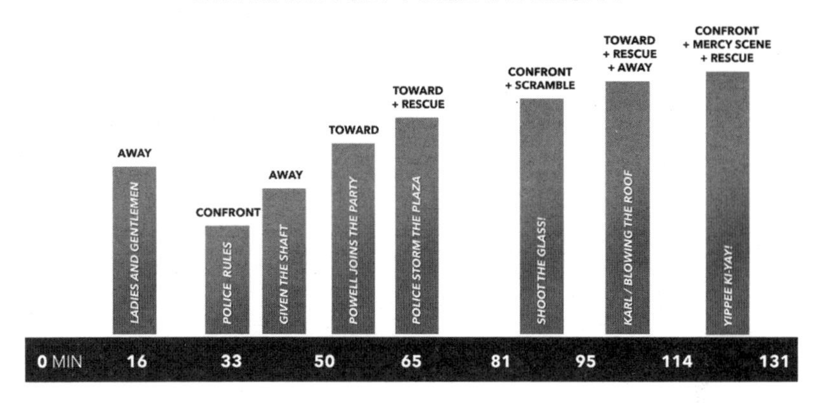

action episodes not only heightens expectation but places emphasis on what comes next. Following each of its kinetic set pieces, *Die Hard* pauses the pace to tighten suspense and stretch tension before pulling the trigger on the next action sequence.

Crosscut Points of View

Die Hard focuses the telling primarily through its hero, but to expand involvement, it crosscuts points of view from Gruber, Gruber's men, Holly, the hostages, the police on the street, and the FBI in the air.

Dynamic Charges

The positive/negative rhythm of Life/Death oscillates with McClane's efforts to rescue the hostages. The closer he gets to saving them, the more positive the charge; the farther away, the more negative.

To build rhythm without repetition, the film's events do not end as they began. When a scene starts with a positive tone, it turns to the negative; when it opens on the negative, it moves to the positive.

Set Piece Movements Merged for Impact

The penultimate action sequence merges three set piece movements (rushing into danger, rescuing victims, escaping danger). The film's climactic sequence melds another three (the mercy scene, final confrontation, rescuing his wife).

Contrasted Tonalities

To modulate intensity, *Die Hard* juxtaposes close-ups of the hostages' terror and the hero's bloody injuries with McClane's jokes and the comic antics of the LAPD deputy chief.

Closing Distances

Excitement builds as hero and villain move from floor to floor, closer and closer, the distance to danger tightening until finally, hands in the air, McClane stands a few feet from Gruber and at his mercy. What's more, the villain holds the hero's wife captive, a gun to her head.

Multiple Values

To deepen impact, *Die Hard* surrounds the core value of Life/Death with a complex of three additional values: Justice/Injustice as Gruber attempts a $100 million theft of the century; Togetherness/Divorce between Holly and McClane; Daring/Fear when McClane faces death.

Deepening Villainy

Hans Gruber first claims to be the leader of a freedom-fighting cause to liberate political prisoners, but when he reveals himself as a sociopathic thief who intends to kill dozens of innocent bystanders, his villainy deepens to the negation of the negation: evil disguised as good. (See *Story: Substance, Structure, Style, and the Principles of Screenwriting*, Chapter Fourteen.)

Progressive Risk

As the film unwinds, impact builds as life-and-death risks accelerate. At first Gruber only threatens the hostages in Nakatomi Plaza and seems content to simply contain McClane. Locked in a labyrinthian skyscraper, McClane calls in the police, but the SWAT team fails, forcing him to hide. Danger rapidly widens to involve not only the LAPD but also the mayor, the FBI, and McClane's wife.

As McClane becomes a greater and greater threat to Gruber's plan, the villain's crew is forced to hunt him down. When they find him, things get personal for the criminals as McClane kills Tony, the brother of Gruber's cohort, Karl. The overall progression to the story's win/lose, all-or-nothing climax follows the universal principle of saving the best for last as Gruber plunges thirty stories to the sidewalk below. The curtain comes down on a resolution scene that lets Officer Powell resolve his long-overdue guilt.

CONCLUSION

Composers not only put notes on a score but also indicate how they are played—forte or piano, staccato or legato, crescendo or decrescendo, and the like. The same holds true for the novelist. Sketchy scenes void of detail seem vapid, while overly verbalized images clutter the mind. As you word-paint images on your reader's imagination, strive for a vivid balance between too little and too much.

Screenwriters face a similar dilemma. Since the invention of the screenplay, Action choreography has been argued two ways: Write it or leave it. Some fill pages with every punch and parry; most simply write "They fight" and let the stunt director stage it. As often as not, less is more and *They fight* gives a production team all it needs to do its best work. If, however, you have an excellent idea for a never-seen-before set piece or stunt, by all means put it on the page.

Thus, two suggestions:

1. When writing an action sequence for the screen, focus on the forces that turn the scene, illuminate characters, and create excitement. You don't need to spell out where every fist lands or what sparks a car fire. Instead, specify the actions that reverse the scene's charge of value. Be clear who wins the conflict and whether she outsmarts or overpowers the loser. Above all, when describing action, no matter how sparse or full, make the turning point clear.
2. Which writer seems more likely to imagine an original scene: one who writes, "Two jets dogfight" or one who researches the effect

of g-forces on fighter pilots and uses that insight to turn the scene in a surprising way? Research each set piece's setting, looking for objects and behaviors no one else has ever seen. Give the stunt director inspirational insight into tactical choreography by visualizing specific weapons of specific use.

In the final step, put action into words.

16

DEPTH AND BREADTH

Once the pace of your story progresses from first page to last, go back to the beginning and explore the possibility of taking your work into greater depth and breadth than you first imagined. As you polish and revise scene by scene, give thought to enhancing meaning, emotion, and impact. Let's take these three one by one.

1. MEANING

When an Action writer has something to say, what exactly is that *something*? Where do you find it? Is that something an idea or a feeling or the two at once? How can you give your Action Story both insight and intrigue?

Poets intensify meaning with enriched language; storytellers intensify meaning with enriched events. In fact, cinema, games, and cartoons can tell powerful tales word-free.

All coherent stories express one irreducible meaning: *how and why life changes*.

Meaning flows beneath settings and scenes, below talk and noise. In emotion-fueled stories, imagined or factual, authors express their vision in their design of events, in their shaping of the forces of cause and effect that underpin the scene-by-scene sequencing of what happens in what order for what reasons. A specific story, therefore, takes root in the subtext, in the hidden sources that emanate from within the setting, cast, and protagonist himself.

Life churns due to numerous causes—some subconscious, some personal, others political or even astronomical. These motivating forces drive characters to make choices, take actions, and cope with reactions. As they do, a value at stake in their lives such as Freedom/Slavery, Truth/Lie, Justice/Injustice, or Life/Death pivots dynamically from negative to positive or positive to negative. Therefore, a story's meaning can be phrased in a single sentence that connects motivating cause to value change.

Meaning in Action

Three examples:

Die Hard: Faced with certain death (negative), the hero invents a brilliant ploy (cause) that kills the villain and saves the victims (positive effect). Therefore, imagination under pressure triumphs over death (meaning).

Guardians of the Galaxy: Confronting an all-powerful being (negative), the heroes resolve their petty differences, unite in comradery (cause), and vaporize the villain moments before he kills billions (positive effect). Therefore, the power of friendship defeats evil (meaning).

Mission: Impossible—Ghost Protocol: Battling through obstacle after obstacle (negative), IMF's ingenious heroes persist (cause) until they finally defeat the villain's plan and rescue the world from nuclear holocaust (positive effect). Therefore, the willpower to persevere saves humanity (meaning).

Nothing like the above is ever said aloud by any character in any Action Story. What characters *do* makes meaning.

Weak writing explains ideas; strong writing expresses insight through a choice of events. *Spider-Man* says, "With great power comes great responsibility." But his well-intended moral message is not the meaning of any of his films. Rather, they all mean this: When a courageous, web-swinging, masked vigilante, toiling outside the law, outsmarts and overpowers villainy, life is rescued from death.

An Action Story's truth hits home in the last act's climax, sending the audience's mind back through the telling to connect the dots, to link cause with effect and grasp the hows and whys of what finally happened. Your audience may or may not put your idea into words, as I did in the last examples, but that doesn't matter. What matters is that your story rings true and feels right so they *experience* your meaning.

An Action Story's meaning may be visceral but never shallow. All express how and why life continues or terminates.

One writer might focus on how an obsession for revenge makes human beings inhuman (*Moby-Dick*). Another may say survival depends on ingenuity and tenacity (*The Underground Railroad*). A third writer conveys how fellowship helps us survive the horrors of war and suicide (*The Lord of the Rings*). In each case, an author expresses an idea, turning point by turning point, by arcing change in a value's charge.

Notice that almost all Action examples end on the positive. What matters is how and why a story gets to its climax. To create Action with originality, first invent heroes and villains who use never-seen-before tactics. Then focus on singular settings and conflicts that create one-off problems for both. Finally, dream up solutions using resources and powers only you can imagine. And above all, tell the truth about power.

The Tyranny Myth

The rationale for all tyrannical systems from Fascism to Communism to Imperialism argues that human beings are the helpless victims of corrupt, invisible forces. As a result, society rots in moral decay, always on the verge of anarchy. To order chaos and restore morality, the people must surrender their power to a strong, noble leader.

To propagandize this idea, tyrants have perverted the Action Genre into a myth that depicts a leader descending from above, killing bad people, saving good people, and then ascending back to a heavenly home.

This myth is a lie and always has been. The Hitlers of history never leave. Once despots seize power, they enforce tyranny, destroy heroes and innocent alike, torch the world as far as they can reach until they finally die, like Franco and Stalin, peacefully in their sleep.

Be wary. Ignorance of subversive Action myths risks perpetuating them. In fact, exposing their lies often motivates superb writing.

Rudyard Kipling saw firsthand how empires believing in myths of superiority have subjugated peoples across the globe. In his *The Man Who Would Be King*, two hero-villains travel to a distant land where they offer mercenary services to tribal chieftains, telling them that their country is weak, but if they give them men to train into an army, they will make the tribe strong again, and then leave in peace. But, of course, they stay, gaining power and, with that, wealth.

At the beginning of *Batman V Superman: Dawn of Justice*, Batman fears the devastating aftermath of Superman's battles with other superbeings.

So, the Caped Crusader decides to murder the Man of Steel. At the same time, Superman finds himself trapped in a moral crisis. He knows that, like a tyrant, he imposes his will across the globe. No government can hold him to account. He enforces what he unilaterally feels is good and inflicts himself on those he decides need punishment. The only thing that stops Superman from becoming a tyrant is his innate altruism.

The Take-Away

To achieve originality, create never-seen-before causalities.

In virtually all Action Stories, the hero triumphs. Because the happy ending is a near-universal effect, wannabe Action writers often feel that the genre leaves them little choice but to follow trends. So, they imitate past devices and try to disguise their clichés.

What separates fascinating Action from pulp is an original vision of how and why what happens, happens. Brilliant authors create heroes and villains who do things in ways no one has ever seen before. Gift your characters with unique talents and tactics to do what they must in ways no one expects and yet seem absolutely believable. Unique causes pay off with inspired effects, so that endings, happy or tragic, climax with shock and surprise.

2. EMOTION

Chapter Five examined excitement, the core or constant emotion that Action readers and audiences feel throughout the telling. But inside that global energy, specific, moment-by-moment emotions surge through storygoers as they react to specific turning points.

All emotion begins with empathy. Audiences want to experience Action by proxy, *as if* it were happening to them...but not really. The personal qualities of imagination and openness in the individual reader or audience member set the depth of their vicarious experiences, but identification with fictional characters is, to some degree, a universal human trait. So, during opening scenes, audiences and readers seek a sense of "like me." They look for a character who mirrors their humanity, who reflects a positive quality they feel within their innermost self. In the Action Genre, that character is almost always the hero.

An audience in empathy with a hero comes to know what he wants and roots for him to get it. What's more, the audience senses how close or far he is from reaching that desire. Once linked by a mutual sense of identity, the audience's emotions pulse with change. As the values at stake in a hero's life (Life/Death, Justice/Injustice, Power/Weakness, Loyalty/Betrayal) change charge from positive to negative to positive and back again, emotion ebbs and flows dynamically through the audience.

Emotions surge during the transitions. As the hero works closer and closer to his desire, the switch from a negative to a positive charge creates an uplifting feeling. Conversely, as forces push the hero further and further from his goal, the transition from positive to negative causes a downward rush. Thrills as the hero moves toward rescue; chills as he's driven away. An event design that constantly shifts the direction of change keeps emotions alive; a repetitious pattern kills them.

The Law of Diminishing Returns decrees that the more and more often an emotion repeats, the less and less its effect. For the fiction writer, this law enforces the rule of thirds: (1) The first time a scene causes an emotion, it impacts with full effect. (2) If the next scene causes that same emotion a second time, the effect will be half or less than half of its original effect. (3) If the telling attempts to cause that same emotion a third time in a row, the effect will reverse and trigger the opposite emotion.

If you compose three negative scenes in a row, the effect will not be tragic/tragic/tragic but tragic/gloomy/comic.

In the first scene, the audience might shed a tear; in the second they may feel sad; but in the third they will smirk and laugh. The first two scenes so drain them of their grief that they have no tears left to give the third. Instead, they now find it annoying that the writer thinks they'll cry yet again. And so, no matter what happens, they find the scene ludicrous and risible. In fact, repetition is a comedy technique known as *reductio ad absurdum*.

The Take-Away

Repetition kills. Jeopardy for victim and hero must build not only progressively but dynamically. Do this: Put your story in a step-outline and track its value charges scene by scene, sequence by sequence from the hero's point of view. Discover whether turning points alternate between positive and negative or bunch together. If the latter, break up the clusters and restructure. Also check to see if events top one another from beginning to end. Does intensity increase in ever-rising cycles or decrease and spiral down? If the latter, once again, redesign the order of events.

3. DEEPENING IMPACT

When you cannot sleep, what goes through your weary mind? Racing thoughts. Nonstop worries, fears, angers, lusts, and dreads rip through your imagination. You constantly replay whatever failed that day into the way it *should* have happened; you rewrite its dialogue into what you *should* have said; you plot the next round hoping you'll finally get it right; and on and on it goes. When at last you fall asleep, your mind shifts into the dream mode.

Dreams compact streaming frets and regrets inside the odd if not bizarre images we call symbols. Dreaming does this to keep us asleep. If not, if images become too real, as they do in nightmares, we wake up and once again rushing thoughts curse us with insomnia.

Symbolism originating in humanity's dream life became embodied in all aspects of culture—art, religion, politics, history. Compared with literal images, symbolic imagery impacts meaning and emotion for two reasons: One, a symbol concentrates an idea's multiple, virtually uncountable variations inside a single image and holds them down out of sight. Two, symbols invade the subconscious mind and, once there, release deep inner energies.

Stories and their imagery work like dreams. They, too, invade the subconscious mind, where they compress meanings and emotions into great intensities. If, however, audiences or readers recognize a symbol as symbolic, if they become conscious of its subliminal nature, if they rationalize its hidden meaning, if they see it for what it is, a storytelling device, its impact vanishes.

To strengthen the impact of your Action Story, create an *image system*: a category of imagery that repeats throughout your telling as a subconscious intensifier of meaning and emotion.

First, select a single species of sights and sounds that you feel relates to your characters, conflicts, and settings, such as machinery, animals, documents, weather, things tabooed, things sacred, or things magical. Then embroider objects and sounds into your descriptions, actions, and dialogue so that your system repeats with great variety and subtlety but never calls attention to itself.

An image system only deepens an audience's thoughts and feelings if it is subliminal. So most important, constantly vary your images. Repeat but never seem repetitious. If, for instance, your image system is "The Garden," you don't want the same willow tree casting the same shadow over the hero every time he pauses to think.

Three examples:

Alien merges the Sci-Fi, Horror, and Action Genres, tying all three together with an image system of *sexual violence*. Phallic or vaginal images infest virtually every scene. To plant its eggs, the monster penetrates its victims orally. A hatchling then chews its way out of the victim's belly in a hideous parody of birth. As it runs off, it looks like an angry red penis on a skateboard. The movie contains three scenes of virtual rape.

The sequel, *Aliens*, took on a new image system of *motherhood*. Ellen Ripley becomes the surrogate mother of Rebecca "Newt" Jordan, the lone survivor of an alien massacre who carries a baby doll wherever she goes. The two are up against the mother of all aliens, a monstrous egg-laying creature that lives in a womblike nest. At a key point, Ripley says, "The monsters make you pregnant."

The image system of *The Hunger Games*, in both the trilogy of novels and the four-film series, begins with the title. The noun *game* has two meanings: a sport to be played for victory and a prey to be hunted for food. The story's imagery combines the two meanings inside a lethal televised sport played by a hero who hunts human game while the game hunts her.

The Take-Away

To deepen the experience of your audience or reader, let your imagination wander through your story's cast, setting, and turning points. Be open to a theme that echoes through the events, an archetypal idea that ties characters and conflicts together. With that as touchstone, express it in sight and sound with the refrains of an image system.

PART 4

ACTION SUBGENRES

Every genre raises a *major dramatic question* that asks a variation on "How will this turn out?" Readers or audiences naturally expect the answer to make sense within the limits of the genre's subject matter. However, when enough stories within a genre refocus that question in a new, unexpected way, these works gather into a subgenre of their own.

The MDQ of the Crime Genre, for example, is "Will the criminal be discovered and punished?" The subgenres of Crime refocus this question through the lens of the protagonist's profession. Cop? Lawyer? Reporter? Gangster? Master sleuth? Master criminal?, and so on, and it therefore becomes: "How will this particular protagonist reveal and punish the criminal?"

The Love Genre asks, "Will love succeed or fail?" Its subgenres raise more specific questions about the stage of the lovers' relationship: "Will they succeed or fail in their romance? In their marriage? In their sexual obsession?"

If a source of conflict is unlimited or vague, anything can happen; a story that allows anything ends up saying next to nothing. So, like Love and Crime, Action calls on subgenres to focus conflict.

All Action Stories raise the general MDQ, "Will the hero defeat the villain?" Action's four subgenres make that question specific to the villain's source of power: the physical forces of nature, the massive power of social institutions, the diabolical powers of individuals, and the unstoppable force of time.

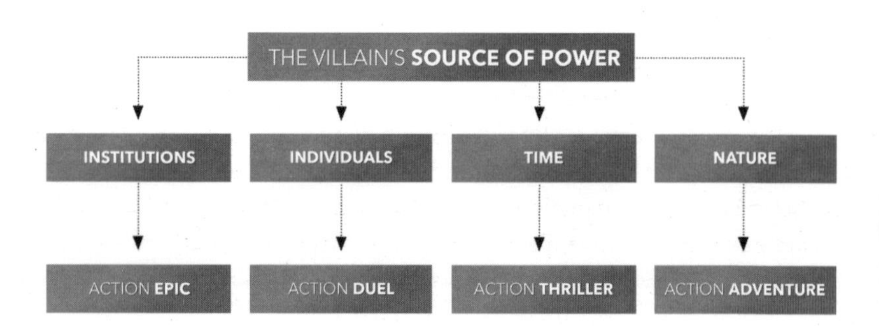

By choosing one of these four sources of antagonism, the writer chooses one of the subgenres of Action: Action Epic, Action Duel, Action Thriller, or Action Adventure. Choice of subgenre shapes a story's spine of Action, guiding the author's creativity and the expectations of his reader/audience.

These four subgenres are endlessly malleable, merging and mixing in yet-to-be-imagined ways. In fact, the subgenres themselves have become so popular that each of them has refined its focus in a variety of ways. As a result, each has within itself four intra-subgenres that further sculpt its sources of conflict. Let's look at Action's four subgenres and their sixteen variations.

17

ACTION ADVENTURE

Action Adventure pits mankind against nature.

When a hero turns a blind corner into an unknown world, pulses pound. Of the four basic techniques for arousing excitement, sending a character into a dark, nameless realm often seems the most electrifying. Unexplored settings range from the murky swamps in *Beowulf* to a galactic nebula in *The Wrath of Khan* to vast Arctic wastes in *The North Water.* Add in all the deadly creatures that inhabit these worlds.

For Action Adventure to hold story-long interest, an author must first invent a setting with never-seen-before powers hidden in its depths, and then devise surprising revelations of how these unique forces work.

In this subgenre, nature can take on any role, except hero.

How an author casts the setting determines which of the four intra-subgenres shapes the telling: Disaster, Monster, Doomsday, Labyrinth.

INTRA-SUBGENRES OF ACTION

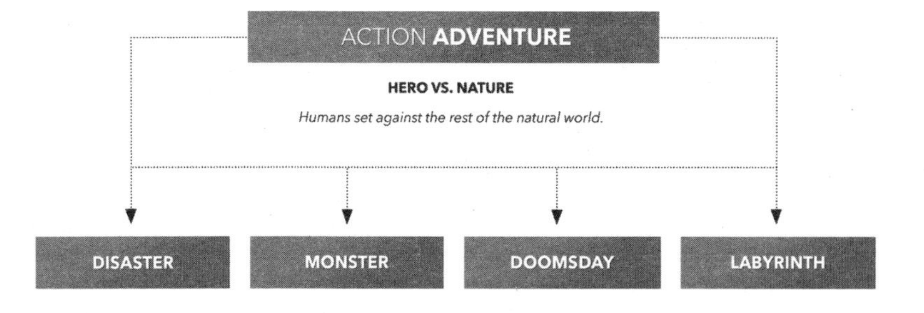

THE DISASTER PLOT

The setting plays villain.

INTRA-SUBGENRES: **ACTION ADVENTURE**

THE DISASTER PLOT

*The **setting** becomes the **villain**.*
The environment seems to possess
*a **conscious purpose** and **lethal scheme**.*

In all Action Stories, the villain's plan drives the telling. The Disaster Plot casts nature as villain, giving the environment a conscious purpose and lethal scheme to carry out.

When left on its own, nature is majestically stable. Storms, forest fires, and earthquakes are simply its way of rearranging the furniture. But human transgressions can provoke nature's darkest intentions. Without a sense of purpose, nature's randomness would splinter a story's spine of action and, with that, erase its meaning. So, to express intention, the writer designs a series of calamities that from an objective angle may seem coincidental, but from the subjective point of view of cast and audience seem focused, deliberate, and deadly.

The merging cyclones in *The Perfect Storm*, for instance, seem aimed at a particular fishing boat, wanting to trap it and swallow it in a deadly tempest. When Captain Billy Tyne sees a mountainous wave swell and block his crew's only way out of the storm, he gives it person and purpose as he remarks, "She's not gonna let us out."

The principles that govern the tactics of Action villains, such as immunity to the hero's weapons, also underwrite the physical forces of Disaster Plots. Nature always has a tactical advantage over the hero.

In *All Is Lost*, the sea slowly strips Robert Redford's yachtsman of anything that could save his life. In *Unstoppable*, every effort to stop a runaway train makes it speed all the faster. In *Armageddon*, when astronauts try to blow up an Earth-destroying asteroid, it fights back with rock storms and bursts of hydrogen gas. In *127 Hours*, the jaws of the rock fissure that captures canyoneer Aron Ralston break the tools he uses against them, turning the film into a hundred-minute mercy scene.

THE MONSTER PLOT

A beast plays villain.

INTRA-SUBGENRES: **ACTION ADVENTURE**

THE **MONSTER** PLOT

***Beasts** become the **villains**.*
*Apex predators sit atop the **natural institution***
*known as the **food chain**.*

When Action casts setting as villain, the telling loses a key source of malevolent power: institutions. The Monster Plot solves this problem by turning nature into an institution known as *the food chain*. Predators sit at its apex, enjoying the villainous tactics that structural power provides. The shark in *Jaws* bends the food chain to its dark purpose, snacking on vacationers and enjoying their terror.

In *The Grey*, the hero leads survivors of a plane crash through a wilderness. As a pack of wolves picks up their trail, the cast's speeches in praise and mockery of the villain shape the climax. The hero applauds the intelligence and savage beauty of the wolves, while the soon-to-be victims mock them, laughing as they throw a decapitated wolf's head at the pack. The wolves growl and howl in a rising anger. The terrified survivors finally realize that in this realm, the wolves wield power, not them.

THE DOOMSDAY PLOT

The setting plays victim.

INTRA-SUBGENRES: **ACTION ADVENTURE**

THE **DOOMSDAY** PLOT

*The **setting** becomes the **victim**.*
Ecosystems, even planets and their entire populations, find themselves in peril.

Nature usually provides a setting, but as seen in the two previous intra-subgenres, it plays the villain with ease. And because the environment today is clearly at risk, the same is true for the victim role.

The Doomsday Plot pushes existence beyond death to extinction. Death flows in a natural cycle from life to death to life again. Extinction breaks that cycle. Which is worse: killing a thousand rhinos or killing the last rhino?

In *Up*, the villain Muntz hunts a rare South American bird. He wants to capture it alive as a scientific trophy, even though its chicks cannot survive without their mother. His egomaniacal lust to prove the bird's existence threatens to drive the species to extinction.

The Doomsday Plot can victimize ecosystems as large as a writer can imagine. In the novel *FernGully: The Last Rainforest*, Hexxus tries to destroy an entire rain forest—plant, animal, human. In *Avatar*, all life on the planet Pandora face extinction. In the animated *Transformers: The Movie*, Unicron, a massive robot, consumes whole planets.

THE LABYRINTH PLOT

The setting becomes a weapon.

INTRA-SUBGENRES: **ACTION ADVENTURE**

THE **LABYRINTH** PLOT

*The **setting** becomes a **weapon**.*
*Hero, victim, and villain are **split up** or **forced together**.*
*The hero must **navigate** through / around numerous barriers.*

A labyrinth can pry hero, villain, and victim apart or force them together. As the hero navigates into or out of its passages and barriers, rescue of the victim becomes more and more difficult and dangerous.

A labyrinth can be as enormous as the ocean or as minuscule as a fishbowl (*Finding Nemo*). The hero of this intra-subgenre seldom interacts with the villain because the environment keeps them apart.

Die Hard: McClane's primary source of conflict is Nakatomi Plaza—its thirty-plus stories, glass windows and partitions, corridors and doors, air vents and security systems. The hero navigates this labyrinth, alternating between keeping himself out of Gruber's sight and killing Gruber's men before they kill the hostages. Gruber alternates between finding McClane and confining McClane.

Die Hard's set pieces weaponize the setting as each floor comes uniquely armed. In a rooftop scene, McClane battles a helicopter, then survives an explosion by jumping off the building, using a fire hose as a trapeze, before crashing through a window. When Gruber realizes that McClane is barefoot, he covers the floor with smashed glass.

This use of a setting became a microgenre for the next few years as writers pitched ideas such as "*Die Hard* in an airport" (*Die Hard 2*), "*Die Hard* on a bus" (*Speed*), "*Die Hard* in the White House" (*Olympus Has Fallen*).

18

ACTION EPIC

The Action Epic pits a hero-as-rebel against the state. In this subgenre, political or social hierarchies take on roles. Rebellion, a key method to arouse excitement, then structures the whole telling. Almost every action the hero takes violates a law or breaks a social taboo.

When institutions become the source of conflict, they motivate one of four possible dynamics: A tyrannical society plays the villain's role, a villain wields an institution like a weapon, society becomes powerless, or society becomes victim.

INTRA-SUBGENRES OF ACTION

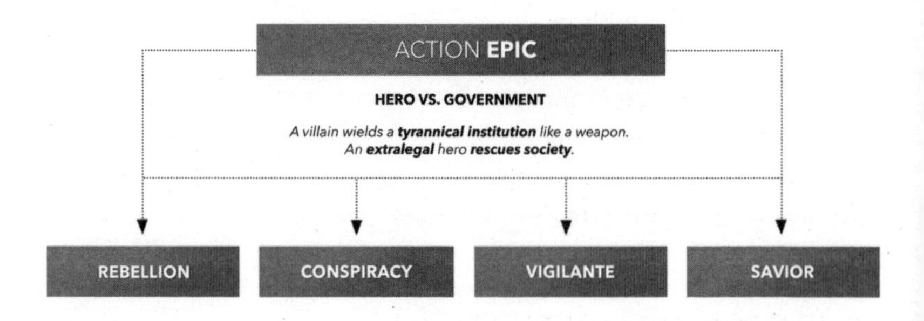

The Action Epic, therefore, offers an author four intra-subgenres: Rebellion, Conspiracy, Vigilante, Savior.

THE REBELLION PLOT

INTRA-SUBGENRES: **ACTION EPIC**

THE **REBELLION** PLOT

An institution is ***corrupt*** *from* ***top to bottom****.*
Extends *the reach and power of villainy.*
Forces the hero to kill ***everyone*** *in his path.*

In this intra-subgenre, corruption fouls a vast institution from leader to minion, top to bottom, creating a massive, multidimensional villain. Setting a story inside a corrupt institution pits the struggle for Freedom versus Slavery against a social architecture. The actioneer must invent a wide-ranging, in-depth pyramid of power, design a cast of roles at all levels, then conduct the flow of commands and tasks from pinnacle to ground and back again.

In *The Hunger Games*, not only does the lavish Capitol of Panem extend its depraved reach into the twelve improvised districts that surround it, but its decrees force the hero to kill everyone in her path.

The Matrix extends its vast villainy via a computer-simulated reality. The villain is not inside the Matrix; the villain is the Matrix. The weapon wielded by Agent Smiths is the delusion of reality. Neo, Morpheus, and Trinity fight a mind-warping battle for freedom against machines that transform all humanity into slaves oblivious of their slavery. Neo, the hero-MacGuffin rebel, fights to bring down this world, yet Agent Smiths seem indestructible and omnipresent. What's more, any individual in society can transform into an Agent Smith at a moment's notice.

THE CONSPIRACY PLOT

In the Rebellion Plot, the hero kills, as he must, the officials and agents of a corrupt institution. In the Conspiracy Plot, however, the hero protects these people. He combats them as necessary but avoids killing them because he knows they're innocent.

INTRA-SUBGENRES: **ACTION EPIC**

THE **CONSPIRACY** PLOT

*The villain uses an **innocent institution** as a **weapon**,
exploiting the **ignorance** of those people inside.
The hero therefore **protects** these people.*

In the Rebellion Plot, villainy saturates an entire institution. In the Conspiracy Plot, the villain uses an institution as a weapon, exploiting the people inside who have no idea that their leader is evil.

In Robert Ludlum's trilogy of *Bourne* novels and the films made from them, Jason Bourne goes to great lengths not to kill the police sent to capture him. They are, after all, unwitting puppets. The Conspiracy Plot, therefore, often conceals a hidden villain whose mysterious identity and string-pulling devices intrigue the audience.

THE VIGILANTE PLOT

INTRA-SUBGENRES: **ACTION EPIC**

THE **VIGILANTE** PLOT

*The hero tries using **institutional authority** as a weapon.
The villain is **immune** to society's rules and
forces the hero to also **break the law**.*

This intra-subgenre reverses the tactical relationship of the Conspiracy Plot. At first, the hero of a Vigilante Plot tries to use the legal system as a weapon against the villain, but the villain, immune to any authority, forces the hero to break the law.

In *Lethal Weapon*, two police officers, Riggs and Murtaugh, pursue the leader of a drug ring until—frustrated by bureaucracy and regulations—they turn in their badges and become vigilantes.

The Vigilante Plot often merges with the Crime Genre, blending the values of Life/Death with Justice/Injustice, turning citizens into Action heroes. Some recent examples: *Harry Brown*, *The Brave One*, *Promising Young Woman*, *Man on Fire*, and *The Equalizer* films starring Denzel Washington.

THE SAVIOR PLOT

INTRA-SUBGENRES: **ACTION EPIC**

THE **SAVIOR** PLOT

*The villain turns an **institution** into a **victim** needing rescue, forcing the hero to rise up as the **people's champion**. These victims create the very **obstacles** the hero must overcome.*

In these stories the villain attacks society at large, turning its institutions into victims needing rescue and forcing the hero to suit up as the people's champion.

This intra-genre often stars a citizen savior, a protagonist of everyday anonymity who conceals a doppelgänger with superlative powers who in turn constantly faces this irony: The society of victims he tries to save persistently create the very obstacles he must overcome.

The Dark Knight pits Batman against the Joker in a battle for "Gotham's soul," but he must also confront the broken morality of the city's citizens and their frenzied mobs.

The Savior Plot invites numerous secondary values: War/Peace, Civilized/Uncivilized, Order/Chaos. But the other three intra-subgenres of the Action Epic also embrace contradictions such as Freedom/Slavery and Justice/Injustice. None of these secondary values, however, are mandatory or exclusive. Life/Death is always at the core of Action.

19

ACTION DUEL

The Action Duel ignores society and its institutions to ignite face-to-face conflicts that pit one against one.

What would be lust for social power and greed for wealth in another subgenre becomes grievances, grudges, and personal vendettas in the Action Duel.

INTRA-SUBGENRES OF ACTION

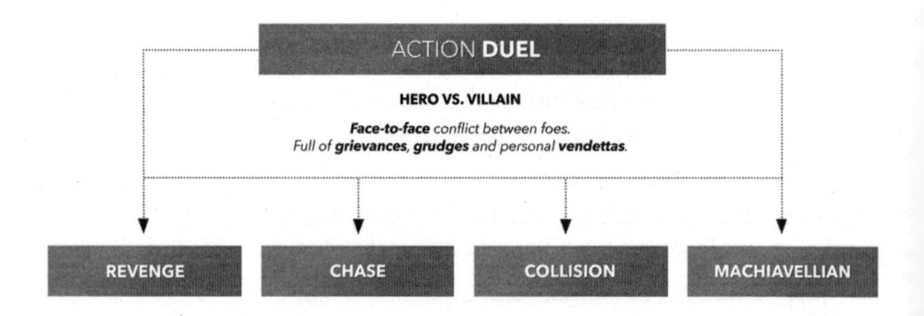

The chief source of excitement in this subgenre springs from delays and barriers that frustrate two hate-filled characters as they circle each other, drawing closer and closer in a spiraling duet of death.

The dark motivations and strategies of these dueling characters create the four intra-subgenres within the Action Duel: Revenge Plot, Chase Plot, Collision Plot, Machiavellian Plot.

THE REVENGE PLOT

INTRA-SUBGENRES: **ACTION DUEL**

THE **REVENGE** PLOT

The hero strives to restore a personal ***sense of honor*** *that was* ***violated*** *by a villain who has gone* ***unpunished*** *by the law.*

Anthropologists divide civilizations by the major system they use to control behavior: law versus honor. When legalities wane, honor waxes. Without strong institutional systems, the public's sense of Justice/Injustice personalizes into Honor/Dishonor. The hero of the Revenge Plot strives to restore a private sense of honor that was violated by an egregious villain who has gone unpunished by the law.

The villain may have a gang (*Taken*, *Kill Bill*), but the lone hero perseveres no matter the odds. Indeed, the villain's depraved, repulsive deeds propel the hero forward as almost every set piece sends her against masses of henchmen while a private rage boils in her depths.

Outwardly, the Revenge Plot may follow the hero, but as in all Action Stories, the villain drives the spine of action. A hero pursuing a passive, inactive villain will not excite, no matter how vile the villain's previous transgressions. Even if the villain has gotten away untouched in the past, the hero must stay active, otherwise she seems undermotivated as she thrusts herself into lethal dilemmas.

In *13 Assassins*, honorable samurai seek revenge against a grotesque despot. The preening, malicious emperor, seemingly untouchable and unaccountable, continuously and sadistically torments his subjects. His endless depravity spurs the samurai into steadfast action.

THE CHASE PLOT

This intra-subgenre reverses the Revenge Plot. Here a villain's enormous physical and tactical powers turn the hero into a fleeing victim.

INTRA-SUBGENRES: **ACTION DUEL**

THE **CHASE** PLOT

The villain's enormous ***physical*** *and* ***tactical powers***
turn the hero into a ***fleeing victim***
who must rescue him/herself.

The hero-victim in a Chase Plot (for example, Ellen Ripley in *Alien*) must rescue herself, continually moving away from danger as the villain pursues. Action/Sci-Fi and Action/Horror mergers find a natural home in the Chase Plot.

The Wrath of Khan pits Kirk against Khan in the backwaters of space, stranded far from the safety of Federation territory. Villains like Khan have no time for institutions or the lure of tyranny. Rather, they crush anyone or anything between them and their prey.

When the Chase Plot combines with a Conspiracy Plot, the villain dupes society into pursuing the hero: *The Fugitive.*

If the setting of an Action telling does not provide institutional power, an author must invent weapons and tactics that turn scenes in new, complex ways. The villain in *Terminator 2*, for instance, has an enormously varied arsenal at his disposal.

Mysterious villains like the Predator keep their chase tactics secret until they suddenly attack. The surprised reactions and instant improvisations by the escaping hero propel excitement scene after scene.

THE COLLISION PLOT

A Revenge Plot sends its hero toward its villain; a Chase Plot drives its hero away from its villain; the Collision Plot sets two heroes against each other in a face-to-face duel. This design poses three major problems: motivation, empathy, balance of power.

1. Motivation

Why would one good guy kill another good guy? Heroes, to be heroic, must risk their lives. Because heroes won't kill each other, an argument

INTRA-SUBGENRES: **ACTION DUEL**

THE COLLISION PLOT

*Two **heroes** are set **against each other** in a face-to-face duel, often **instigated** by the villain.*

between them might risk Friendship versus Enmity but not Life versus Death.

Avengers, *Avengers: Age of Ultron*, and *Captain America: Civil War*, three recent Collision Plots, resorted to misunderstandings and mind control to motivate their confrontations. Mind control first appeared on-screen in *Dracula* (1931), and misunderstandings have hinged every Romantic Comedy that ever featured a tap-dancing Fred Astaire. When honestly motivated, however, a Collision Plot's duel to the death can feel inescapable and exciting.

Looper found a unique solution by arcing roles: In this time travel adventure, two versions of the same character collide. The younger starts the telling as a villain, the older as a hero. Then, as the story progresses, their roles gradually arc in opposite directions.

Troy worked both designs. The Atreus brothers, Agamemnon and Menelaus, orchestrate a war that forces two heroes, Achilles and Hector, to collide. In time, however, the glory-hungry Achilles turns so dark in spirit that the audience welcomes the arrow that pierces his defenseless heel.

2. Empathy

If two heroes draw equal empathy, would an audience find a Collision Plot exciting? Doubtful. Rather than rooting for one versus the other, audiences might hope that the two heroes come to their senses, but if, like Achilles and Hector, Batman and Superman, they persist, excitement melts into regret.

3. Power

The balance of power in the Collision Plot is also problematic. Heroes are underdogs to villains, not each other. A stalemate of simultaneous underdogs seems absurd.

In *Batman V Superman: Dawn of Justice*, Lex Luthor's machinations shift the balance of power between the heroes dynamically. At first, Superman, the vastly more powerful of the two, subdues Batman. But then Batman uses Luthor's secret stash of kryptonite to turn the tables until he has the Man of Steel at his mercy.

THE MACHIAVELLIAN PLOT

INTRA-SUBGENRES: **ACTION DUEL**

THE MACHIAVELLIAN PLOT

*Two **villains** are pitted **against each other**,*
*while the hero struggles to bring down **both of them**.*

The Machiavellian Plot inverts the Collision Plot and pits two villains against each other while the hero struggles to bring down both.

This two-pronged story design poses some risks.

Audience indifference: If two villains turn against each other, who cares? Their deaths would save the hero the trouble and the lives of at least two victims.

Audience confusion: If the villains don't turn against each other and instead force the hero to pursue the two of them, each of whom pursues a personal scheme, each scheme aimed at a separate object of desire, each needing a different MacGuffin to achieve it, the storytelling splinters into two unrelated spines of action.

Audiences and readers expect unity. Years of storygoing experience have taught them that every word, image, and action in a story somehow relates to everything else in the story, either causally or thematically or both. No matter how intriguing a text may seem, an audience seeks linkages of cause with effect, of contrasting correlation in the subtext. In the Machiavellian Plot, for instance, they instinctively expect that the two story lines will somehow mirror each other and join before the telling ends.

Split spines of action can unify within a Machiavellian Plot in three ways: by giving two villains the same goal, or the same MacGuffin, or both.

In *Star Trek into Darkness*, for instance, two villains hunt very different targets but fight over the same MacGuffin. The superhuman Khan Noonien Singh captures a shipment of cryonically frozen super-soldiers because he wants to create an uber-society of genetically engineered beings. At the same time, Alexander Marcus, a renegade Starfleet admiral, wants this force so he can start a war against the Klingons.

In this fourth intra-subgenre, the hero faces a dangerous balancing act: If his attacks on one villain draws the attention of the other, then two villains coming from different directions at the same time will be unstoppable. Even worse, the two villains may realize that if they team up, they can overcome the hero with ease. Yet to play one against each other, the hero must take that risk.

A Fistful of Dollars, the remake of the Japanese classic *Yojimbo*, pits the protagonist against a town ruled by two despotic gangs. These gangs respect each other's boundaries, creating virtual hell for the townspeople. The hero worms his way into each gang, manipulating them into fighting the other, but when the hero's deceptions are outed, he finds himself up against the firepower of both gangs combined.

20

ACTION THRILLER

The Action Thriller pits the hero against a ticking clock: never enough time, never-ending time, time as a weapon, time as a victim.

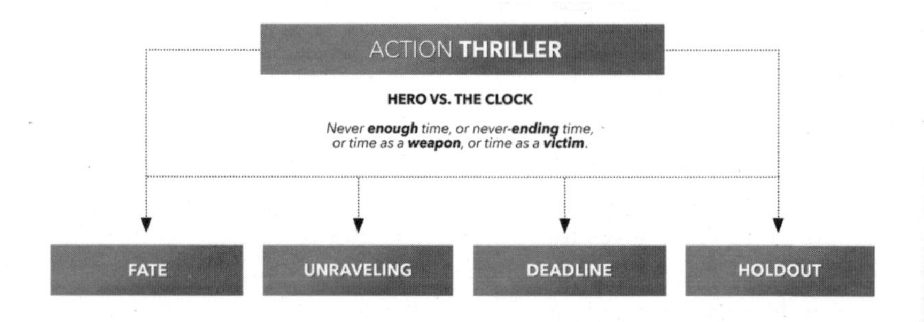

Hours, minutes, seconds spin high-tension excitement as they ensnare the hero in temporal traps.

Time is the name we give to change. From day to night, season to season, life to death, the universe and everything in it changes. We call this process of measurable change *time.*

Time holds an imperial power over human beings: We are its subjects; it rules us; we kneel to it. Time may pass slowly or quickly or, in fantastic worlds, go backward or forward or sideways into an eternal dream realm. But in life, the choice of time's direction and purpose is beyond our control.

Nature adapts; time persists. We often think of nature as alive with purpose, sometimes a lethal intent, but we rarely see time as a living thing that reacts to our actions. However, when an Action Story grants purpose to time, what seemed random, meaningless, and benign becomes deliberate, meaningful, and villainous. Time governs reality and we bow to its majestic first law: *All things must change.*

Choice of the role, pace, and purpose of time shapes the four intra-subgenres of the Action Thriller: Fate, Unraveling, Deadline, Holdout.

THE FATE PLOT

INTRA-SUBGENRES: **ACTION THRILLER**

THE FATE PLOT

Time becomes the ***villain****.*
When time compels a ***negative ending****, we call it* ***Fate****.*
The hero tries to ***stop*** *Fate.*

In the Fate Plot, time becomes a villain.

When a story begins, we instinctively look into its future to sense the hero's *Destiny*. Hope gives that destination a positive glow. But when a story climaxes and we look back on its links of cause and effect, we realize that the characters, out of their inner natures, chose the only actions they would have chosen. What's more, the world, out of innate necessity, reacted in the only way it could react. We now reflect on the hero's *Fate*, often with a somewhat negative connotation because the path of events seems inexorable. The Action hero of a Fate Plot defies this sense of inevitability by rebelling against time and its law of change.

In *Back to the Future*, Marty McFly travels back in time and accidentally changes the past. Time begins erasing him from history as he struggles to right his mistake. We realize that time's intensions are lethal when it removes Marty's older siblings from a photograph, one by one.

THE UNRAVELING PLOT

INTRA-SUBGENRES: **ACTION THRILLER**

THE **UNRAVELING** PLOT

*Time becomes a **victim**.*
*When time brings about a **positive ending**, we call it **Destiny**.*
*The hero tries to **save** Destiny.*

In the Unraveling Plot, time becomes a victim.

In the Fate Plot, a hero tries to stop his Fate. In the Unraveling Plot, a hero tries to save his Destiny.

If we believe that time has no life of its own, it cannot die. But if we imagine time the way we imagine nature and grant it an active purpose, it becomes a living thing that can be killed. The Unraveling Plot casts time as a vulnerable victim—a past, present, and future that face annihilation.

In the Fate Plot, time plays the villain, pursuing its purpose with a driven, relentless, tenacious determinism. No matter what you do, time drives toward your Fate.

The Unraveling Plot reverses this. Time as victim becomes so fragile and malleable that the death of a sparrow could ripple with consequences through time/space that completely rewrite a thousand years of civilization.

In *Back to the Future*, time nearly kills Marty, but then in *Back to the Future, Part II*, Biff Tannen, the series villain, kills time and erases Hill Valley's bliss-filled small-town Destiny, transforming the happy hamlet into a decadent, crime-ridden hell.

In *Men in Black 3*, the heroes, Agents J and K (both young and old), and the villain, Boris the Animal (both young and old), take turns killing decades of time, each trying to create the future they prefer.

X-Men: Days of Future Past: Wolverine goes back in time to avoid a nightmarish genocidal future. But as he interacts with the past, the course of history unravels, and the nightmare accelerates its pace. Key events that lead to destruction happen decades earlier than they're meant to; risk grows with his every action and reaction.

THE DEADLINE PLOT

INTRA-SUBGENRES: **ACTION THRILLER**

THE DEADLINE PLOT

Time becomes a ***weapon****.*
The villain sets a ***precise limit*** *that traps the hero.*

In the Deadline Plot, time becomes a weapon.

Virtually all Action Stories exploit time to some extent, but in this intra-subgenre the villain weaponizes it by setting a precise limit that traps the hero inside the villain's plan. As seconds count down, the Deadline Plot steadily erases the gap between now and then, turning scenes faster and faster, the tempo quicker and quicker, shifting kinesis into overdrive as the hero juggles multiple tasks in less and less time.

Every set piece in *Mission: Impossible—Ghost Protocol* sends the IMF team racing against time to stop World War III. Because they can't wait for backup or take a breather, they must match tenacity with ingenuity. Because they have no chance to fix a mistake, the pressure of getting it right the first and only time heats each scene white-hot.

Limited time limits choice; limited choice inflicts unlimited jeopardy. In *The Dark Knight*, the Joker threatens to blow up two crowded ferryboats at midnight. He gives the passengers, however, a way out: In each boat he has planted the detonator to explosives on the other boat. Whoever pulls the trigger first lives. Otherwise, the passengers and crews of both boats will perish when the clock strikes twelve.

In *Tenet*, an omnicidal villain invents a technology that reverses entropy and thus enables time travel. He vaults into the future in search of an algorithm that can reverse entropy for the entire planet. Once he has that power, he plans to erase all living things from the face of the Earth, humanity first and foremost.

THE HOLDOUT PLOT

INTRA-SUBGENRES: **ACTION THRILLER**

THE **HOLDOUT** PLOT

*Time becomes **magnified**.*
*Time is **stretched** to torture the hero for what seems like eternity.*

The Holdout Plot magnifies time into a massive, limitless setting.

All Action Stories combine narrative drive (looking forward) with suspense (holding your breath). The Deadline Plot erases time to push narrative drive into the future. The Holdout Plot restrains time to squeeze out every last drop of suspense as it tortures the hero for what seems like eternity.

All Action set pieces combine tension with kinesis. The Deadline Plot thrives on kinetics, but the Holdout Plot favors tension, dramatizing the depths of a hero's endurance and grit, seeing how far he can stretch his dwindling resources. Most of all, the Holdout Plot questions, as the title suggests, how long he can hold out.

Aron Ralston, the hero of *127 Hours*, carefully rations everything he has, including his urine and his sanity, to outlast the hours in the film's title. Mads Mikkelsen, as the hero of *Arctic*, not only endures an endless trek across polar wastes but tows a wounded pilot on a sled behind him.

21

MIXTURES AND MERGERS

Genres mix when a story line in one genre crosscuts with a story line in a different genre. The hero of an Action Story could also be the protagonist of a Love Story, with the telling splicing back and forth between them.

Genres merge when one genre blends into another by giving it a deeper motivation. Again, a hero could be the protagonist of both an Action Story and a Love Story, but in a merger of the two, the hero's lover becomes the story's victim, and so the hero pursues the villain *because* she's in love. Now the Love Story drives the Action Story.

Action subgenres and intra-subgenres can mix and merge, even if they seem contradictory. *Edge of Tomorrow* merges the Holdout Plot with a Deadline Plot. Major William Cage dies in a battle against aliens and then wakes up back in his staging area faced with a deadline for the battle that just killed him. He reenters the same fight in a temporal loop. Again and again, he relives and re-dies, holding out to become a better and better warrior while forced to face endless deadlines.

What's more, Action can crosscut with any of the other principal genres of outer change. *Back to the Future*, for instance, combines its Action story line with a Family Drama and a Love Story. Action/Crime mergers, such as *Lethal Weapon*, cast protagonists as detective-heroes. An Action/Crime hybrid, such as *Ant-Man*, redeems a criminal by turning him into a hero.

The merger of principal genres offers unlimited storytelling possibilities but, at the same time, raises questions of balance, emphasis, and focus: How much of one genre? How little of the other?

MIXTURES VERSUS MERGERS

The core value of Action dramatizes Life/Death, and so the genre mixes easily with principal genres that also focus on external values, such as Justice/Injustice in the Crime Genre, Power/Weakness in the Political Drama, Freedom/Tyranny in the Modern Epic, and Victory/Defeat in a War Story.

But when an Action telling delves into the psychological complexities of its hero, outer conflicts stir inner dilemmas of Morality versus Immorality, Belief versus Unbelief, Maturity versus Immaturity, and the like. In those emotional depths, the audience's empathy for the hero deepens, turning excitement into anxiety. So, the question for the writer becomes, "How much excitement will my story lose if I merge it with an arc of inner change?"

The mixtures and/or mergers of principal genres demand balancing acts of key story elements. When two genres combine, which core event deserves the most emphasis? The core event of the Crime Genre is the revelation of the criminal. When Crime and Action merge, does this reveal come before or after the mercy scene?

In *The Bourne Identity*, the mercy scene traps Bourne in a French country house. His escape and execution of a hired assassin climaxes Act Two. Later in Washington, DC, the reveal of the villain turns the Third Act climax.

MODAL GENRES

As outlined in Chapter One, the media of screen, page, stage, and video game generate modal genres.

Onstage Action is the least common because kinetic theatricality is not only difficult but also dangerous, as seen in the many injuries suffered by the cast of *Spider-Man: Turn Off the Dark*. On the other hand, song and dance in the Musical can motivate kinesis with great effect, as *The Lion King* proved.

The comic book and graphic novel illustrate kinesis, while prose descriptions project rapid images in the reader's imagination. Action, however, whether animated or live or interactive, finds its most natural home on the screen.

Even so, some filmmakers feel that editing makes action feel contrived, and so to make fights more convincing, they film them in a single take. Jackie Chan, sufferer of countless injuries on set, has been known to do over a hundred takes to get his kinetic effects to work.

Comic book originals have traveled through graphic space and time to fight intergalactic despots for almost a hundred years. In recent decades, they found live-action success on screen thanks to CGI-filled images that mine the rich history of these hand-drawn characters and give them what they always implied but never had: motion.

European comic strips and the video games adapted from them—*Valerian, Tintin, Asterix, XIII, Lucky Luke*—also have a century-old tradition. As do the Science-Fiction sagas of Japanese manga: *Akira, Ghost in the Shell, Attack on Titan, Fist of the North Star.* All have been recycled on-screen as series-length or feature-length animations.

TEMPORAL GENRES

Stories differ greatly in performance time, and so the temporal genres sort them into short form (less than an hour of performance or less than a hundred pages of reading), feature form (one to four hours or from one hundred to four hundred pages), and long form (a telling that needs more than one sitting to experience, and therefore requires at least one break).

Length of performance determines complexity of story, variety of characters, number of set pieces, and budget. Short-form Action calls for the smallest cast, simplest plotting, least budget, and usually limits set pieces to one or two. Feature form expands on those limits, while the extreme performance times of long form demand more and more of all four elements. Long-form telling, whether over a series or sequels, imposes the greatest creative demands on the Action author.

The first difficulty a creator faces in long form comes the second, third, fourth, or fifth time she asks the same reader/audience to reconnect with the same hero. What will capture interest again and again? What's new? Answer: the source of evil.

Villainy is far more inventive and flexible than heroism. Heroism, after all, is a moral reaction to evildoing. Without bad guys, there would be no need for good guys. Batman is very fortunate in that regard. His decades-long run has been made possible by the gallery of psychotics stored in Arkham Asylum, madmen who seem to take turns escaping.

If a hero has an ongoing archnemesis, then the mysterious, unattainable MacGuffin they seek must fascinate the audience over multiple installments. In *Star Wars*, for instance, Luke Skywalker and Darth Vader clash over the rule of a galactic empire, but what ultimately matters is command of the Force.

James Bond pits himself against a different villain with each film, but recently they all work for the shadow organization known as SPECTRE. This institutional structure gives the hero the best of both worlds: a persistent all-powerful nemesis who runs a cohort of vile operatives.

Extending an Action hero's adventures over multiple years, even decades, risks repetition and creative exhaustion, but fortunately, the unlimited reinvention of villains and victims, along with mixtures and mergers of genres, subgenres, and intra-subgenres, will keep long form playing forever.

STRUCTURAL GENRES

The vast majority of Action tellings dramatize extra-personal conflicts in a classic archplot. But exceptional event designs such as the minimalism of *All Is Lost* or the anti-plotting of *Monty Python and the Holy Grail* or the multi-plotting of *Game of Thrones* also thrill audiences, so long as they direct their heroes against external antagonisms, rather than inwardly against themselves. (See *Story*, pages 43–66.)

PRESENTATIONAL GENRES

Action Stories can be told through any combination of presentational genres. Chapter One listed ten such styles: Comedy, Animation, Science-Fiction, Fantasy, Historical Drama, Biography, Autobiography, Documentary, Musical, and High Art. These wide-ranging treatments express Action through tonal filters of seriousness versus wit; in various temporal perspectives of past, present, future; fictionally or factually; or with intensified auditory and imagistic designs.

One popular example: Any Action telling can change an audience's experience drastically by turning into a Comedy. Comedy keeps audiences at a safe, pain-free distance. No matter how characters writhe in pain and tremble in fear, blood-soaked, violent scenes in an Action/Comedy whisper, "It doesn't really hurt."

By virtue of an ancient storygoing convention, Comedy makes audiences grin while characters groan. In fact, the surprising, explosive turning points of Action/Comedy trigger the biggest laughs of all. The mercy scenes in *Galaxy Quest*, *Men in Black*, and *Guardians of the Galaxy*, for instance, play out not only the most exciting showdowns but also the craziest jokes.

22

HIGH ADVENTURE

High Art, the tenth presentational genre, expands a story's vision from the particular to the universal. In High Art, the specific meanings of conventional tellings expand into all-embracing truths. Shakespeare, for instance, took a gritty Danish folktale about the mad King Amleth and reinvented it as his masterpiece, *The Tragedy of Hamlet, Prince of Denmark*.

In the Action Genre, High Art becomes High Adventure. High Adventure deepens and enriches the value of Life/Death with themes that expand into social and political realms as well as the human heart. Compare Robert Benchley's vivid, page-turning novel *Jaws* with Ernest Hemingway's sublime telling of *The Old Man and the Sea*—one was a best-seller and hit film, the other won Hemingway the Nobel Prize; one lost our interest decades ago, the other will live for centuries.

As an Action cast fights for their lives on the text, the High Adventure author invites the reader/audience into the subtext of these characters and their worlds. He then intensifies the telling with an image system that arcs the telling from the typical to the archetypal.

HEIGHTENED MEANING

High Adventure engages character-rooted values. To Action's extra-personal value of Life/Death in the physical realm, High Adventure adds inner conflicts of Morality against Immorality, Compassion versus Indifference, Mercy warring with Cruelty—the evolution or devolution of a character's humanity.

In most Action Stories, good triumphs over evil as the hero outwits and/or overpowers the villain. High Adventure, however, widens outward into humanity, even to transcendent, universal themes that raise the grandest questions of meaning and purpose.

To reach these heights and depths, High Adventure intensifies its tellings with symbolic image systems.

HIGH ADVENTURE: ACTION AS **METAPHOR**

IMAGE SYSTEM

*Category of **symbolic** imagery that **repeats** with great **variety** and **subliminal** subtlety. Intensifies a story's **meanings** and **emotions** **subconsciously** in the reader/audience.*

Physical settings burgeon into archetypes: City streets become *The Labyrinth*, a waterway becomes *The Sea*, a stretch of rough land becomes *The Desert*, back alleys become *The Underworld*, a tropical island becomes *Paradise*, a home becomes *The Palace*, a rocky peak becomes *The Sacred Mountaintop*.

These epitomes then link with other images throughout the telling to form an image system that repeats with great variety and subtlety throughout a story to deepen and enrich its meanings and emotions. As noted in Chapter Sixteen, this ongoing pattern of motifs must be subliminal. During a story's performance, readers and audiences must never become consciously aware of symbols and their significance. The moment an image system jumps off the page or screen and calls attention to itself as *art*, its power vaporizes into snobbery. The time for intellectual discussions comes after the film, not during.

CHARACTER COMPLEXITY

The same intensification applies to the characters in High Adventure. The separate qualities of altruism, narcissism, and helplessness in the conventional core cast become self-contradictory, multidimensional, and psychologically complex in High Adventure.

High Adventure's bigger-than-life characters embody human nature it all its moral and spiritual contradictions. Heroism often mixes with villainy as a protagonist becomes his own worst enemy. These hero-villains frequently become their own victim as well. As they confront a fate of their own making, their inner complexities fascinate audiences and readers, arousing an emotional cocktail of excitement, pity, and dread.

The climax of High Adventure often inflicts a tragic irony on its hero: He triumphs but also loses something of great value, or he fails but also gains something superlative, such as wisdom. From the point of view of readers and audiences worldwide, the finest tellings of High Adventure transcend the delights of entertainment to become life-enriching works of art.

THEMATIC COMPLEXITY

As explored in Chapter Two, the dynamic, straightforward, core value of Life/Death drives the Action Genre. Its meaning is clear and singular: alive and moving in the here and now versus dead and buried and gone for good—Existence/Nonexistence.

High Adventure intensifies this value into Immortality versus Damnation. Life has a biological limit; immortality extends it into eternity. Death is final but damnation never ends. For souls suffering in Hell, going out of existence would be a mercy. In the Horror/Action film *Constantine*, for instance, the hero descends into Hell and discovers suffering souls longing for escape into nothingness.

Although Life/Death always hangs in the balance, High Adventure often adds other values to enrich the telling. The hero's outer struggle to save a victim may become a metaphor for his inner fight to save himself from a spiritual or moral death. Seeking even deeper values, High Adventure may evolve or devolve the character's innate being as a suspense-filled audience/reader wonders if the hero's adventure will ultimately enrich his humanity or erase it.

Here are some examples:

The North Water

This Action Adventure series adapted from Ian McGuire's novel dramatizes the full spectrum of nature's cruel indifference—human and animal on land and sea. From vomit-spewn waterfront alleyways to ice-choked Arctic seaways, values compound as the Life/Death of survival couples with Justice/Injustice in a Crime Story subplot and the protagonist's arc to a fulfilled humanity in his Evolution Plot.

Game of Thrones

This long-form Action/Fantasy tells an immense Action Duel between an idealistic fanatic (Daenerys Targaryen) and a realistic autocrat (Cersei Lannister). These two take the opposite sides of the series' dominant value: Freedom/Oppression.

The Matrix

At first, the hero believes that he lives in the 1990s, but he wakes from this false reality to discover that, in fact, he lives somewhere in the twenty-first century. Artificial intelligence now rules a post-apocalyptic Earth and uses human beings as its energy source. It placates the mind by trapping it inside a computer-simulated dream existence—the Matrix.

As the protagonist evolves from Mr. Anderson the victim to Neo the hero, his arc mirrors the personal struggles of the film's creators, the transgender Lana Wachowski and Lilly Wachowski. Both felt imprisoned in socially dictated identities not their own. The anonymity of the internet, however, gave them a choice of gender free from physical and social constraints. Inspired by online anarchy and their need to find a true self, they wrote *The Matrix* and imbued their film with a core value of True/False Identity.

INTENSIFIED MEANINGS

Any of Action's four subgenres and their sixteen intra-subgenres can aspire to High Adventure. A story's meaning intensifies to the archetypal in three ways: Characters develop dimensionality, a subliminal image system deepens its impact, and its values expand its meaning beyond Life/Death.

Consider these four examples:

Action Duel / Chase Plot: *The Terminator* by James Cameron

ACTION DUEL: THE **CHASE** PLOT

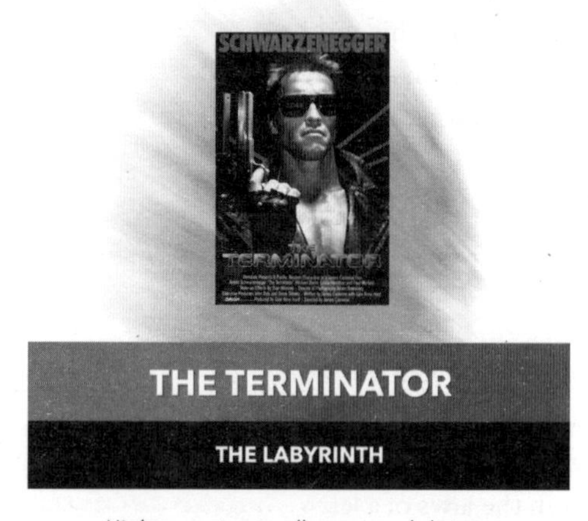

Highways, streets, alleyways, cul-de-sacs and corridors of buildings form a ***maze*** *through which the* ***villain chases hero and victim****.*

Cast

A time-traveling, multidimensional assassin known as the Terminator is outwardly calm yet inwardly raging, indifferent to his wounds yet vain about his appearance, and most important, a living contradiction—a machine-human hybrid.

John Connor, the commander in humanity's war against sentient machines, sends Kyle Reese, his young lieutenant, back in time from 2029 to 1984 Los Angeles on a mission to rescue Connor's mother, Sarah. The Terminator wants to kill Sarah before she gives birth to John Connor, thus eliminating humankind's leader from existence and giving victory to AI in the coming Armageddon.

Image System: The Labyrinth

Cameron based his telling on the Greek myth of Theseus versus the Minotaur, a hybrid man-bull monster lurking in a maze created by the master engineer Daedalus on the island of Crete. Ariadne, a Cretan princess, falls in love with Theseus and gives him the secret he needs to stalk the beast to the heart of the maze, slay him, and escape the labyrinth.

Like Theseus and Ariadne, Kyle and Sarah fall in love, make love, and she becomes pregnant with Reese's son, John. In other words, the father of the future savior of humanity is the young lieutenant that the leader sends into the past to save his mother. This warping of cause and effect wraps the Connor family in a temporal web.

In pursuit of his target, the Terminator kills every woman named Sarah Connor in the LA phone book. But before he can kill the last on his list, Reese rescues her. Hero and victim flee and the chase begins.

The film's image system turns the streets, alleyways, highways, cul-de-sacs, and corridors of buildings in Los Angeles into an elaborate labyrinth reminiscent of the one from Greek myth. Villain, hero, and victim twist and turn their way through a rat's warren of dead ends, circling down and down into the guts of a factory. There, Reese sacrifices his life so Sarah can win the final battle. At the epicenter of this maze, she crushes the Terminator in the jaws of a lethal, metal-crushing stamping machine.

Meaning

The events in this film risk the extinction of humanity, intensifying the core value of Life versus Death to Survival versus Annihilation.

It's worth noting that the initials of John Connor, the destined savior of humanity, reference not only the Christian savior but also, coincidentally, the film's creator.

Action Adventure / Monster Plot: *Moby-Dick* by Herman Melville

To dramatize the industrial revolution's desecration of nature, Melville focused his novel on the whaling industry. The crime was of such magnitude that it called for events, characters, and poetics of equal scale.

Cast

Ahab, captain of a whaling boat, seeks revenge against Moby-Dick, an albino sperm whale that bit off Ahab's leg years before. At first the captain

ACTION ADVENTURE: THE **MONSTER** PLOT

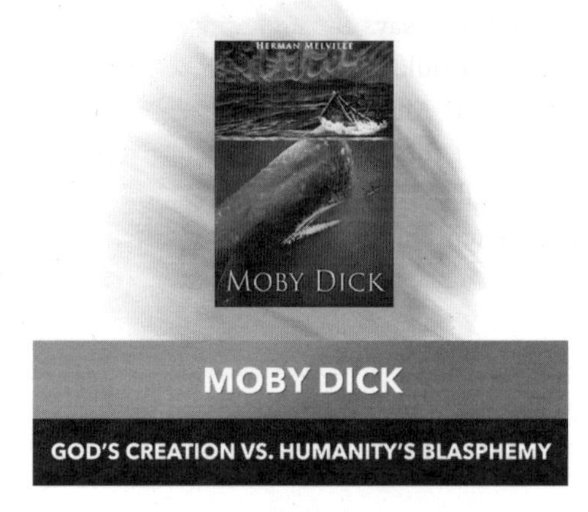

*Nature as God's **divine work** corrupted by the **sacrilege** of human industry.*

seems like a hero-victim and the whale a monster-villain. Over time, however, Ahab turns villain as his obsession mesmerizes his crew until they fall victim in a losing battle against the gigantic Moby-Dick. Seen from a reverse angle, the whale becomes Nature's hero, protecting God's creatures before they fall victim to human destructiveness.

Image System: God's Creation Versus Humanity's Blasphemy

For over 250 years, the industrial revolution has torn nature apart and to this day, still treats it as a slave to be whipped in the service of industry. The whaling industry (as just one example) has killed these stupendous beings by the millions to provide whale oil to lubricate machinery and whale ambergris to make perfume.

To match the magnitude of these crimes against creation, Melville turned to the Old Testament for an image system that portrays nature as an unknowable god, human industry as a corrupt sacrilege, and Moby-Dick as the hand of God. Against him stands the blasphemer, Ahab, with his crew of killers.

Melville opened his novel with a preacher sermonizing on Jonah and the whale. He named his narrator and point-of-view character after

Ishmael, Abraham's oldest son. For his protagonist's name, he chose a king of Israel, Ahab. Of this king the Bible says, "Ahab did more to provoke the God of Israel to anger than all the kings who went before him" (1 Kings 16:33). At one point Ishmael says of the hate-filled captain, "Had Ahab's chest been a cannon, he would have shot his heart upon the whale."

In the climactic fight, Ahab devolves into madness. Harpoon lines strap him to the back of the Leviathan he lusts to kill. As Moby-Dick surges through the swells, Ahab's dead arm seems to wave to his crew, beckoning them to die with him in the vastness of the deep.

Meaning

Melville's novel intensifies Life/Death to the Survival/Annihilation of all living things—not only nature but human life as well.

Action Thriller / Deadline Plot: *Watchmen*, written by Alan Moore and illustrated by Dave Gibbons

The detonation of the first atom bomb ushered in the possibility of human extinction. The Cold War soon followed, and the Cuban Missile Crisis engulfed the world with dread. Decade after decade, despite

ACTION THRILLER: THE **DEADLINE** PLOT

*Life as time **winding down**,*
*history running out and **ending**.*

treaties, nuclear armaments stockpiled higher and higher. The Three Mile Island meltdown was followed by the even greater disaster of Chernobyl. Paranoia gave way to resignation.

In reaction to this history, writer Alan Moore and illustrator Dave Gibbons sensed that superheroes are a simplistic answer for the complex conflicts they aim to solve. So, they looked for hidden possibilities in the psychology and ethos of superheroism. One hero might become insanely obsessed with justice; another could lose purpose and feel impotent. Vanity might seduce the dark impulses of a mighty ego, while humility tempts another to surrender.

To put their insights into action, Moore and Gibbons fractured the Action ideal, unmasked its subconscious motivations, and exposed the cultural assumptions secreted beneath its images and dialogue.

In *Watchmen*, a comic series in twelve issues, they placed their heroes in a twisted alternative 1986 in which Richard Nixon reigns as president and the world ticks closer and closer to nuclear holocaust. The heroes want to avert this catastrophe but with no clear or identifiable villains, they don't know who's responsible or when it's set to happen. What's more, their struggle to avert doomsday merges with inner debates over the meaning of existence and the temptation to resign themselves to the extinction of humanity.

To expose the troubled idealism of the Action Genre, *Watchmen* splinters time, space, events, and characters.

Time

Scenes fly back and forth through nonlinear time, crisscrossing decades of reinvented history as if temporality has no meaning.

Space

Characters teleport from New York City to Mars to Antarctica and back again as if distance has no meaning.

Events

The story starts with a suspicious murder and ends on the threat of incineration of all life on Earth as if social structures have no meaning.

Characters

In *Watchmen*, millions of New Yorkers suffer as victims while each major role portrays a variation on the hero/villain fracture.

Rorschach arcs from a Manichean vigilante to a martyr desperate for heroic death. The Comedian, the cigar-smoking vigilante who rapes Silk Spectre I, goes to work for the government. Silk Spectre II's identity crisis ends when she finally accepts The Comedian as her father. Adrian Veidt (aka Ozymandias) degenerates from the epitome of heroism to the villainous architect of Armageddon, killing half of New York City in his mad scheme to save humanity.

In constructing the character of Doctor Manhattan, Alan Moore wondered if a character living in a quantum universe would perceive time from a linear or cyclical or random perspective. Whichever view he chooses would distort his sense of human affairs. So, Moore arced Doctor Manhattan from a nihilist to a believer in miracles.

All in all, contradictions so riddle these characters that notions of morality and conscience have no meaning. A sense of futility permeates *Watchmen*. Time ticks away in the Deadline Plot, but the characters look toward the Day of Reckoning with listless impotence.

Image System: The Doomsday Clock

The title *Watchmen* begins an image system that refrains on temporality: History running out, hours winding down, life ending. The key image is the Doomsday Clock, a device that measures the time left before global catastrophe. A bloodstained smiley face button echoes this clock and reoccurs in various ways throughout the telling.

Doctor Manhattan, a former clockmaker, can bring himself back to life from the dead and rearrange matter at a whim. This godlike superpower is likened to fixing a clock: knowing the pieces and how they fit together. His ability to see the future acts like a countdown. Life becomes a clock face with no hands, no beginning, no end, ticking away until nuclear war breaks the clock.

At story climax, the heroes finally discover the villain's plan but too late to stop it. He executed it thirty-five minutes earlier.*

Meaning

Beyond Survival/Annihilation, *Watchmen* raises the values of Hope versus Despair and Logic versus Absurdity, but it ends in passive resignation to the negative charges of both.

Action Epic / Rebellion Plot: *The Lego Movie* by Phil Lord and Christopher Miller

This unassuming gem, starring toyetic characters, surprised unsuspecting audiences with its depth and candor. Lord and Miller merge the principal genres of Action and Domestic Drama with the presentational genres of Fantasy, Animation, and Live Action to give life-and-death excitement a one-of-a-kind energy.

---

* Sara J. Van Ness, *Watchmen as Literature: A Critical Study of the Graphic Novel* (London: McFarland & Company, 2010).

ACTION EPIC: THE **REBELLION** PLOT

The stifling Lord Business symbolizes the ***perfectionist*** *father, while Emmet does the same for his* ***freedom-seeking*** *son.*

Settings

The film tells parallel stories in two realms: a basement reality where a boy named Finn plays with Legos to create a tabletop town, and the boy's imagination that envisions the fantasy city he calls Bricksburg.

Cast

The boy's father (aka The Man Upstairs) rules Finn's life; a control-freak tyrant named Lord Business rules Bricksburg. Lord Business wants to glue every moving part of Bricksburg into a rigid permanence that outlaws anything new; the father wants to do the same to Finn's Lego town. In Bricksburg, Emmet (Finn's avatar) rebels against Lord Business; in the basement, Finn, inspired by Emmet, wins respect for his creativity and, with that, a newfound independence from his father.

MacGuffin

The story's two-part MacGuffin plays out in both settings. In Finn's basement world, it's a tube of Krazy Glue and its cap. In his imagined world of Bricksburg, Krazy Glue becomes the Kragle, a superweapon that fuses Lego pieces, and its cap turns into the Piece of Resistance that disarms it.

Events

In the opening sequence, Lord Business attacks the wizard Vitruvius, steals the Kragle, and hurls Vitruvius into an abyss. As the wizard falls, he prophesies that someday a special one will rise up to stop the ruler's scheme and thus save creativity.

Years later, Emmet, a happy-go-lucky construction worker, tumbles into an underworld chamber and discovers the Piece of Resistance. When he touches it, he undergoes a blinding vision of The Man Upstairs and wakes as a prisoner of Lord Business's enforcer, Bad Cop / Good Cop. The heroic Wyldstyle rescues Emmet. Believing him to be the Special, she takes him to Vitruvius.

Emmet learns that Wyldstyle and the wizard are Master Builders—capable of creating anything without instruction manuals. When Emmet reveals his MacGuffin-inspired vision, Wyldstyle and Vitruvius believe that he is the hero who will lead their epic struggle.

A mélange of heroes rally to their cause: the superheroes Batman, Superman, Green Lantern, and Wonder Woman; warriors from *Lord of the Rings*, led by Gandalf; *Star Wars* characters C-3PO, Lando Calrissian, and Han Solo; Abraham Lincoln; Shaquille O'Neal; and Shakespeare.

Emmet leads this united force against Lord Business, but despite their combined powers, Lord Business captures the hero, kills Vitruvius, and imprisons the Master Builders. After throwing the Piece of Resistance into the abyss, he sets his tower's self-destruct mechanism and leaves everyone to die.

In this mercy scene, the ghost of Vitruvius suddenly appears to Emmet and tells him that to become the Special, he must believe in himself. Emmet then pulls the battery out of the self-destruct mechanism and straps it to his back. Facing death, he flings himself off the tower and saves the lives of the Master Builders.

Emmet then wakes to find himself in heaven: Finn's basement. At this point, reality and fantasy join as Finn's father comes down the basement steps to chastise his son for mixing playsets.

When the father starts gluing Legos together, Emmet sees the danger and gets Finn's attention. Finn quickly places Emmet and the Piece of Resistance in the tabletop town. Emmet, now back in Bricksburg, confronts Lord Business.

At the same time, Finn confronts his dad. Using the speech Emmet gives Lord Business, Finn tells his father that he has the power of creativity. Suddenly, his father realizes that Finn based the villain on him. Shamed, he reconciles with his son.

Meanwhile, in the fantasy world, Lord Business also has a change of heart. He caps the Kragle with the Piece of Resistance and unglues his victims with mineral spirits.

The two parallel Rebellion Plots build Finn's Maturation Plot. These three story lines motivate the Redemption Plots for the villainous Lord Business and the stiff-necked father, arcing both from cruel to kind.

Image System: Father/Son as Ruler/Rebel

The film's image system is a hall of mirrors. Two worlds, real and fantasied, reflect each other, as do the stifling Lord Business and the perfectionistic father. Reverse images pit the rule-driven father against the liberty-seeking son.

The Lego Movie tells an Action Fantasy built around an image system that recasts father and son as Ruler versus Rebel. In the boy's imagination, Emmet Brickowski, his animated avatar, battles Lord Business, a figure symbolizing his father, aka The Man Upstairs. The fantasy's image system of Creative Freedom versus Rigid Dictatorship mirrors the eternal power struggle between a rule-making father and his freedom-seeking son.

This imagery builds to an emblematic climax when Emmet dies and goes to fantasy heaven—a basement with real people. The creators of allegories can set their rules any way they like, so these filmmakers bend their setup to join real and fantastic realms in a magical blend that elevates this Action Comedy to High Adventure.

Meaning

Phil Lord and Christopher Miller ground their true-to-life clash between father and son in the ageless conflicts of Rebellion versus Obedience and Freedom versus Tyranny. In the end, however, neither the positive nor the negative vanquishes the other.

23

FORM VERSUS FORMULA

We close with a refrain on the introduction, a reminder that form is not formula. A form is a universal that includes every possible example. The Action Genre pits a hero against a villain to save a victim. That's it. All Action fits that form, but its variations are endless. A formula, however, is a limited, rigid subset of the universal that dictates how to execute that form in one limited way.

Some writers, it seems, find the notion of improvisation and reinvention off-putting. To them, the idea of form seems formless. They want a blueprint. What follows are two of the most famous writing formulas in Hollywood history: the Whammo and the Journey.

THE WHAMMO FORMULA

Fifty-plus years ago, researchers at Columbia Pictures analyzed box-office returns and found that hits pivot six to eight major turning points per film as opposed to the conventional three or four. This discovery inspired a new theory for financial success: Explosive reversals sell tickets. Therefore, turn more to sell more.

The studio then devised the Whammo Chart, which formulated major turning points by page count. The studio's story department was instructed to compare every submitted screenplay to this graphic. Those that matched the Whammo Chart were sent on; those that didn't were sent back.

As a result, Columbia, the studio that had won more Best Picture

Oscars than any other, did not make *Rocky, Patton, Raging Bull, The Deer Hunter, The French Connection*, or *One Flew Over the Cuckoo's Nest*. It made neither *The Godfather* trilogy nor the *Star Wars* trilogy. Fortunately for Columbia, in 1980, a new CEO discarded the Whammo Chart, putting the studio back on track.

THE JOURNEY FORMULA

The success of *Star Wars* gave rise to a second formulaic pattern. Following his hit, George Lucas proudly announced that he had cribbed his story ideas from Joseph Campbell's book *The Hero with a Thousand Faces*. The overwhelming success of *Star Wars* convinced Hollywood that Campbell's Hero's Journey was the new key to financial success. Manual after manual has recycled this formula ever since.

The Hero with a Thousand Faces outlined a pattern of events that Campbell claimed was the archetype that underlies virtually all Action myths. Since its publication, however, anthropologists and mythologists have rejected, indeed contradicted, Campbell's claim.

First, they pointed out that Campbell had twisted Otto Rank's *The Myth of the Birth of the Hero* (1932) and Carl Jung's "The Concept of the Collective Unconscious" (1936) in ways both authors would reject. Second, to persuade readers that his claim was true, Campbell simply ignored every case that contradicted him. Third, he also avoided classic Greek and Middle Eastern myths and instead referenced obscure tales from obscure tribes that no one could verify. Fourth, when he needed examples to support his contentions, he just made them up. Finally, his key examples, when subjected to scientific study, become transparent fallacies. In short, scholars with a deep knowledge of myth dismissed Campbell's theories.

Consider the world's oldest Action tale, *The Epic of Gilgamesh*. The protagonist, Gilgamesh, opens the telling as a tyrant, hated by his people. He undergoes a change of heart thanks to his partner in life, Enkidu. Together, the two men set out on various adventures, one of them a quest for immortality, but eventually all their adventures fail. Gilgamesh doesn't return with an elixir of life. He saves no one from tragedy, not Enkidu, not himself. Death has the ultimate power. This truth created a magnificent High Adventure.

Like all storytelling formulas, the Journey commits the categorical error of mistaking the part for the whole. The whole is the universal form of story embedded in the Action genre; one aspect of that is an adventurous quest. Not the other way around.

The Hero's Journey is, at best, the blending of an Action Plot with a Maturation Plot. In *127 Hours*, this merger makes the hero stand still. And that is its point. Formulas reduce Action to a chain link of clichés.

We explored Action's four subgenres and sixteen intra-genres to outline the familiar shapes Action writers have used, knowing, however, that conventions are not rules for writing. Audiences and readers enjoy these patterns but never demand them. To keep Action alive and thriving, master its form, but then improvise and reinvent the genre for future fans. Guided by a sense of creative freedom, let's all embrace our love of Action.

ACKNOWLEDGMENTS

My thanks go to Oliver Brown and Luke Lyon-Wall, who read repeated drafts, gave insightful notes, and never lost faith. And, as always, I thank my editor, Marcia Freedman, and her unerring eye for what makes sense and what doesn't.

INDEX

ABOUT THE AUTHORS

Robert McKee, a Fulbright scholar and member of Final Draft's Hollywood Hall of Fame, is the world's most sought-after author and lecturer known for his seminars/webinars that provide writers with crucial insight on the story universe. His writing seminars have earned him an international reputation. The cornerstones of his teaching are *Story*, *Character*, *Storynomics*, and *Dialogue*. Translated into twenty-three languages, these singular works have defined how we talk about the art of storytelling. Over the last thirty-five years, he has mentored screenwriters, novelists, playwrights, poets, documentary makers, producers, and directors. The list of McKee alumni includes the winners of over sixty Academy Awards, two hundred Emmy Awards, and one hundred Writers Guild of America Awards, as well as recipients of the Pulitzer, Booker, Olivier, and other major prose and playwriting prizes.

Bassim El-Wakil has worked closely with Robert McKee for over a decade, as an author and lecturer. Acknowledged as an expert on all forms of story structure and genre, he has a personal love for Action, Crime, Fantasy, and the long-form serials of television and comic books. His podcasts, The Story Toolkit and The Writer's Jihad, are available on all major podcast platforms.